DIVE
SNORKEL

sites in Western Australia

DEPARTMENT OF CONSERVATION AND LAND MANAGEMENT

Above: Stunning Pocillopora Reef, at Rottnest Island, is easy to reach from shore.
Photo — Gerhardt Saueracker/Lochman Transparencies
Below: Anemonefish are common inhabitants of tropical and subtropical waters, such as Ningaloo.
Photo — Eva Boogaard/Lochman Transparencies

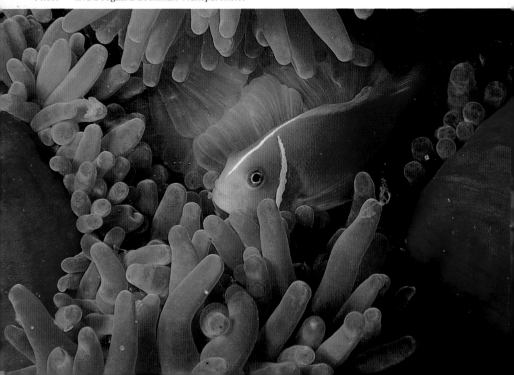

Above: Yellow anemones are common in Marmion Marine Park.
Photo — Dick Beilby/Lochman Transparencies
Below: Port Jackson sharks are common in South-West waters. They are usually harmless.
Photo — Eva Boogaard/Lochman Transparencies

Contents

PERTH AREA

GASCOYNE

Foreword

Welcome to *Dive and snorkel sites in Western Australia*, the Department of Conservation and Land Management's first guide to diving and snorkelling in marine areas. The book is designed primarily for snorkellers and novice divers and there is a strong emphasis on shore dives and dive sites within marine parks.

The main criteria for dives in this book were relative ease and accessibility. We tried to choose dives that were fun and interesting. It is hoped that the information provided about marine life will stimulate your interest in the marine environment and encourage a conservation ethic.

So what are you waiting for - go out and experience the dives for yourselves!

Syd Shea

EXECUTIVE DIRECTOR
Department of Conservation and Land Management

Introduction

ABOUT THIS BOOK

Dive and snorkel sites in Western Australia is designed primarily for snorkellers and novice divers. None of the sites is in depths greater than 18 metres. There is a strong emphasis on shore dives and dive sites within marine parks. However, there are also many boat dives that experienced divers would find challenging and enjoyable and some moderately difficult shore dives.

It was difficult to grade the dives because many dives that seemed "easy" might be difficult in certain weather conditions. Read the information provided about the skill required and caution areas carefully and assess the weather before attempting any dive, even those graded easy. It would be possible to encounter difficulties in almost all of the sites in adverse weather or strong currents. Even a little swell can also affect visibility, so it may be better to wait for optimum conditions.

The mud maps are intended to be used as a rough guide only and are not drawn to scale. Scales and distances given are only approximate. Please do not place too much emphasis on their accuracy and balance the information provided here with your own judgement. Always keep an eye open for potential hazards that may not have been evident when the sites were mapped, and match the dive sites with your level of skill. Your safety is our concern but your responsibility.

CARING FOR THE MARINE ENVIRONMENT

Coral reefs, eerie shipwrecks, caves, limestone harbour walls, tropical lagoons and forests of kelp are just some of the diverse features of Western Australia's underwater world. Each place has its own array of natural wonders. Marmion Marine Park, for example, is home to Australian sea lions. The park's eroded limestone reefs are a diver's paradise, forming ledges, caverns and swimthroughs. They are inhabited by a wonderful array of temperate and tropical fish species and colourful invertebrates. To the north, Ningaloo Marine Park offers a vastly different diving experience. It protects a 260 kilometre long barrier reef that is one of only two large coral reef systems to occur on the western edge of a continent. It is also the only large reef found so close to a continental land mass; about 100 metres offshore at its closest point.

Diving in marine parks

Several important and representative underwater habitats are protected in marine parks, which are managed by the Department of Conservation and Land Management (CALM). There are marine parks at Marmion, Shoalwater Islands (near Rockingham), Shark Bay and Ningaloo (near Exmouth). A number of other areas have been proposed for consideration as marine parks and these waters may be declared as marine parks or reserves at some stage in the future.

The purpose of marine parks is to ensure that their underwater habitat and ecosystems are preserved indefinitely. WA's marine parks are zoned to ensure that users of the park don't impinge on each other's activities. There are three different zone categories.

Sanctuary zones are areas where visitors may "look but not touch". No fishing of any kind is permitted in these areas and all marine plants and animals are totally protected. They serve as benchmark areas to monitor any changes in adjacent areas in which fishing is allowed, and as replenishment zones, which allow new fish to repopulate nearby depleted reef communities in the event of excessive use. They also enable visitors to experience pristine coral and reef communities.

Recreation zones exclude commercial activities but generally permit recreational activities such as fishing, provided that fishing regulations are followed. It is the diver's responsibility to ensure that he or she is up-to-date with current regulations and bag limits, holds any applicable licenses and only takes marine animals such as rock lobsters or abalones during the declared seasons. Regulations may vary from park to park. *General use zones* provide for commercial fishing and other uses that are consistent with conservation. In some cases, *special purpose zones* may be declared to meet the conservation needs of a particular area, if the three zone framework does not fit the situation.

There are also many other beautiful and ecologically significant areas outside marine parks that are heavily used by divers but not at present subject to any management control. It is up to the individual diver to ensure that his or her activities maintain the environment in its natural state.

Other protected areas

Wrecks are protected under an Act which prohibits the removal of artefacts or wilful damage of any sort. Please help preserve our maritime heritage by leaving wrecks undisturbed.

The waters around Rottnest Island are protected by a marine reserve, and no spearfishing is allowed within these waters.

Maintaining the underwater world

Diving can affect unspoilt marine communities in many ways. Activities such as spearfishing, harvesting or collecting marine life may disrupt normal marine communities, by altering the number and diversity of species. Divers can easily select the site and type of fish they wish to take, a practice which can result in exploitation of certain species at particular sites, upsetting the natural balance.

While the impact of one diver may be minimal, many dive sites are visited by thousands. Because it is so easy to reach from Hillarys Boat Harbour, Boyinaboat Reef, a limestone outcrop in the Marmion Marine Park off metropolitan Perth, is visited by up to 100 divers a day during peak summer periods.

Marine manners

Interaction with aquatic plants and animals is both a privilege and a responsibility. When you dive, make up your mind to leave an area as it was before you arrived, avoiding undue disturbance to the marine environment and its resident plants and animals. Leave marine invertebrates where you find them, for all to enjoy, and if you pick up a rock or a shell always put it back where you found it. Virtually anything you pick up will probably have an animal living in it.

Make sure your diving gear is secured and not dangling, and watch where you're kicking: fins can break off coral and other invertebrate life. Good buoyancy control is important so that you don't crash into animals such as corals. You should also take great care when settling on the bottom; quiet, smooth movement is less likely to disturb animals and will let you observe aquatic life behaving naturally, rather than fleeing or hiding.

Follow these simple guidelines and you will be sure to enjoy some wonderful diving!

DIVING SAFELY

SCUBA diving and snorkelling have claimed lives and divers should never become complacent about safe diving practices.

Never dive on SCUBA if you have not completed an accredited course. Many of the sites mapped and described in this book can be explored by snorkelling. You do not have to be a qualified SCUBA diver to learn about and enjoy the marine environment. However, it is recommended that you complete an accredited snorkelling training program.

Prior to diving, ensure you are using the correct equipment for the conditions, particularly if you haven't dived in the area before or if you haven't dived on SCUBA for awhile. Check all of your equipment thoroughly to ensure it is in good working order, ensure you have the correct number of weights and a suitable exposure suit for the conditions. A compass and knife are standard safety equipment. Always carry essential spare parts such as mask and fin straps, O-rings and a first aid kit. Ensuring you have the right equipment on the day will make your dive safer and much more enjoyable.

Always check the weather forecast on the morning of your dive. However, don't just rely on the forecast, and assess the dive site thoroughly before entering the water. If you are uncertain about the suitability of the weather conditions for your planned dive, ask at the local dive shop. They will probably be able to suggest an alternative site if conditions are unsuitable. Be flexible and alter your plans if necessary.

Regardless of whether you are snorkelling or SCUBA diving, always display a dive flag and always dive with a buddy. If diving from a vessel, make sure someone is left to watch the boat (refer to the next chapter on 'Safe Boating'). Before diving, you and your buddy should:
1. Inform a friend of your dive site and your estimated time of return;
2. Establish entry and exit points and techniques;
3. Choose a course to follow, taking currents and other factors into consideration;
4. After consulting dive tables, agree on a maximum time and depth limit;
5. Establish and review communication procedures and revise hand signals;
6. Agree on an air pressure for returning to the surface, usually 50 bar;
7. Decide what to do if separated; and
8. Discuss what to do should an emergency arise.

Before entering the water, ensure you and your buddy run through the five-point equipment check:
1. BCD - needs to be snugly adjusted and operating properly. It should be partially inflated before you enter the water;
2. Weight belt - should be fitted with weight savers, have a right hand release and be free of all equipment and straps;

3. Releases - check to see where they are and ensure they are all secure;
4. Air - check that your buddy's air is turned on, ensure that the regulators are working, note where the alternate air source is and how it is used and make sure the air pressure hoses are not tangled;
5. Final - make a final once over for dangling straps and missing equipment.

Always use an approved dive table and stay within its limits. While diving, keep track of the time, depth, direction, temperature and air supply at all times. And don't forget that at the end of your dive you should ascend slowly and cautiously. A five minute safety stop at five metres is recommended. While ascending, keep an eye out for any boats in the area.

In the event of decompression sickness call Fremantle Hospital at Alma Street in Fremantle, which coordinates the treatment of all cases of civilian diving accidents. Call (09) 335 0111 and immediately state that the call is about a diving related accident. To report a boating accident, or to initiate a search, call Police Communications on (09) 222 1111.

SAFE BOATING

The ocean deserves your greatest respect at all times. Even experienced boaters can occasionally find themselves in serious difficulties. However, if you plan your trip well and take care to observe standard safety precautions you will minimise the chances of any problems occurring.

Always check the weather forecast before you leave and take it into account in deciding where you should go, the load you can safely carry and the people you take with you. Remember that a sea of 1.5 metres is about the maximum for comfort on a trailable-sized boat. This is the approximate wave height that a steady wind of about 15 knots will build up. Cancel the trip if necessary. Keep on eye on the weather at all times while you are on the water, and head for shore if you see a thunderstorm developing. You should also consider accompanying another boat - operating in pairs will increase your safety.

Always carry the minimum safety equipment on board, including:
* a bilge pump (mandatory on boats at least seven metres long, unless they have sealed, self-draining decks), bailer or bucket;
* a suitable fire extinguisher;
* suitable life jackets for each person on board;
* an effective anchor and line;
* two parachute distress flares, approved to Australian Safety Standards;
* two hand-held orange smoke signals or one smoke canister; and
* a two-way marine band radio.

It is recommended that you check with the Department of Transport for current information on the minimum safety equipment to meet legal standards.

To ensure you have a trouble-free and enjoyable trip, check that your boat, motor, fuel system and equipment are in good working order and ensure you are carrying enough fuel. Aim to have at least 25 per cent of your fuel left over, after completing your trip in the worst conditions you can imagine. In addition, make sure you have the correct charts, a compass, water, food, extra clothing, adequate tools and spares, an extra line for the anchor, as well as sunscreen, hats and other sun protection.

Decide where you intend going, your expected time of return, the amount of fuel you will carry and where you intend to launch. Let somebody, preferably the duty officer at the local sea rescue group, know about your excursion and provide them with the names and phone numbers of the people on board, a description of your boat and registration numbers, your car and trailer registration numbers and a list of your safety equipment. If you logged on by radio, don't forget to log off.

When anchoring, it is wise to put out at least three times as much anchor line and chain as the depth of the water you are anchoring in. For example, in 10 metres of water put out at least a 30 metre anchor line. When anchoring close to reefs, consider the effects of sudden wind and sea changes on the position of your vessel. Play it safe and anchor in such a way that your vessel will lie in safe water regardless of such changes. And, of course, be considerate and don't anchor in coral or seagrass areas.

If divers are operating from a vessel they must display a signal to warn other boaters. The dive flag should be at least 750 millimetres long by 600 millimetres wide. The flag signifies that all boats should keep at least 50 metres clear. If this is not possible, then the boat must proceed at the slowest possible speed that allows full control and maintain a look-out.

Never leave your boat unattended. If the anchor line should snap while you are diving below, you will be stranded in deep water (literally).

COBBLERS AND CONESHELLS

Many marine animals use venom or toxins for catching prey or defending themselves. Some of these may cause mild stings or rashes if contact is made with human skin. Only a few species have venoms or toxins potent enough to cause serious harm to people, and these are not often encountered. However, it is best to be aware of any problems they can cause and avoid coming into contact with them.

Blue-ringed octopuses and some species of fish-eating coneshells are among the most dangerous. These creatures kill their prey with a potent toxin injected with their bite, and although such cases are very rare, they have killed people. Blue-ringed octopuses live in reef flats and in tidal pools in muddy areas and can be recognised by their brilliant blue rings when disturbed. Be cautious when handling dead shells and when exploring underwater crevices or caves. Coneshells are conical and cylindrical in shape. They bury themselves in sand by day, and emerge at night to search for small fish, snails or worms. You should avoid picking up live coneshells.

Certain fish, such as catfish (also known as cobblers) and stingrays, have venomous spines and can cause painful injuries. Use common sense around these creatures, as well as toadfish, pufferfish, boxfish and porcupine fish. Although they may appear to be slow-moving and docile, they are capable of inflicting serious bites if handled.

Stonefish are found around the top two-thirds of the Australian coast. They inhabit coastal reefs and shallow mudflats and usually lie partially buried on the sea floor. If people tread on this animal the sharp venomous spines can pierce their feet, causing severe pain and tissue damage. Always wear strong footwear (not thongs) when walking in shallows. Shoes will also provide protection from razor shells, which also inhabit the shallows of northern Australia.

Sea-snakes are also found in marine areas, and some species are extremely venomous. They are quite curious and may approach, but if you don't touch them they should leave you alone. Bristleworms (ringed or segmented worms up to 20 centimetres long) often lie under rocks or in corals. Their bites may cause injury. So can the bristles, if they penetrate the skin. Be wary if turning over rocks or corals.

Sharks are also common inhabitants of our coastal waters and some species are dangerous. As with other potentially dangerous fish, don't be tempted to touch them, as they may try to defend themselves by biting.

In tropical areas, such as Ningaloo Marine Park, fire coral is found on the sand around reefs and fireweed can be found growing on the reefs. These marine organisms can cause a burning sensation. Wearing gloves and protective suits will avoid stings from accidentally brushing against them.

If you are unlucky enough to be bitten or otherwise poisoned by a marine animal, keep the injured limb still and seek immediate medical attention. However, most marine animals should not pose a problem unless harassed or inadvertently touched or trodden upon. Fortunately, most injuries can be avoided by simple common sense and behaving cautiously around any animal or plant that you are unsure about.

SOUTH-WEST

Leeuwin-Naturaliste Coast

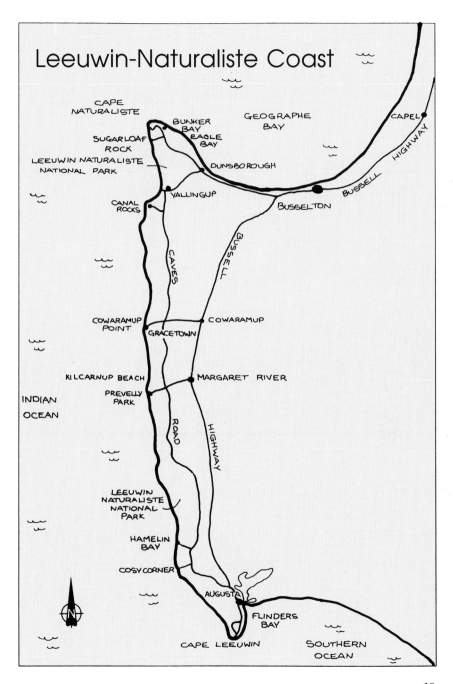

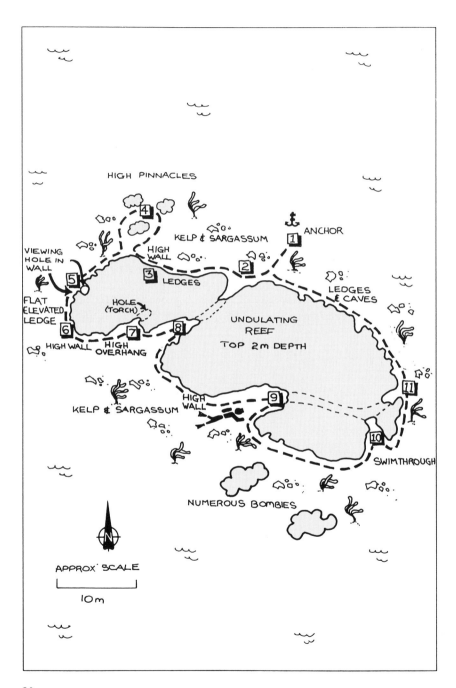

HIGH PINNACLES

KELP & SARGASSUM

4

ANCHOR

1

VIEWING
HOLE IN
WALL

HIGH
WALL

2

5

3   LEDGES

LEDGES
& CAVES

FLAT
ELEVATED
LEDGE

HOLE
(TORCH)

UNDULATING
REEF

TOP 2m DEPTH

6

7

8

HIGH WALL   HIGH
OVERHANG

HIGH
WALL

11

KELP & SARGASSUM

9

10

SWIMTHROUGH

NUMEROUS BOMBIES

N

APPROX SCALE

10m

Flinders Bay bombie

How to get there: By boat from the Flinders Bay boat ramp, south of Augusta.
Depth: 10 metres.

This bombie is half a nautical mile south-south-east from the western end of
Seal Island, on a true bearing of 148 degrees. Seal Island, the closest island to the
mainland, is located south-east of the Cape Leeuwin lighthouse and south of Groper
Bay.

From the western end of Seal Island, proceed in a south-south-easterly direction, keeping the first large granites that protrude above water level to your left. The
second group of granites, formed in a crescent shape, should also be kept on your
left. The bombie lies in the cup of the crescent, in open but semi-sheltered waters.
(Take care, as submerged reefs and other bombies lie en route.)

1. Depending on the wind direction, anchor to one side (usually to the north). The
   bottom is rock and kelp, so it is best to use a reef anchor. After you descend to
   the kelp bed below, your depth gauge should read ten metres. Look towards the
   bombie, where you will see a huge diversity of marine life.
2. The wall of the bombie rises almost vertically for eight metres, interrupted often
   by caverns, ledges and overhangs. You will be greeted by a blaze of soft corals and
   sponges (some pale blue in colour), together with fish species such as maori
   wrasse, prettyfins, black-headed pullers, leatherjackets and footballer sweep.
3 & 4. Swimming in an anti-clockwise direction, harlequin fish and scalyfin peer
   curiously from cavernous openings in the wall. As you follow the maze around
   to the western end of the bombie, look to the north, where high pinnacles and
   numerous small bombies rise from the kelp and sargassum. Here you are likely
   to see blue groper, banded sweep, herring, buffalo bream and old wives.
5. On a good day the clarity of the Southern Ocean will astound you, as you feel the
   influence of a gentle surge. Near the southern end of the western side of the
   bombie there is a round port hole in the reef wall, which resembles a looking
   glass.
6. Follow the wall to the southern side of the bombie, where an elevated reef
   platform juts from the wall at medium-depth, as if placed there as a viewing
   platform. Sea sweep often hover nearby.
7. Further around to the left, a rounded cave entrance halfway up the wall
   continues in to a narrow cavern, where torch light is needed to reveal a

fascinating variety of life. Nearby there is a high overhang, covered in a mass of multi-coloured marine organisms such as gorgonians and sponges.

8. A large cave opens in to a swimthrough where red-lipped morwong, rough bullseyes, foxfish and wobbegong might be seen. Follow the high, sheer wall and look closely at the fascinating diversity and colours.

9. Another cave forms an interesting swimthrough, where you are likely to see western blue devils and brightly-coloured sea stars sheltering under ledges. To your right, numerous small bombies loom from the kelp, with interesting low ledges.

10. At the eastern end of the bombie a cavern opens in to yet another swimthrough, linking with another further around. Here, truncate coralfish and long-finned pike may be observed.

11. Further to the left, a series of ledges and small caves can be explored, returning you to the point adjacent to your boat. Here, slate pencil urchins, boarfish and plate coral top off one of the best 45 minute dives you may ever experience in temperate waters.

Caution areas: Access to this site should only be attempted in slight to moderate sea conditions. Surface currents may be present in these areas and should be checked before commencing any dive. Watch for submerged reefs en route.
Degree of difficulty: Moderate to difficult, depending on conditions.
Area's status: Proposed marine park.

Peter Lambert and Andrew Horan with assistance from Ted Wright

SEAL OF APPROVAL

The New Zealand fur seal is found close to Augusta and other parts of Australia's southern coast but, as its name suggests, it is found in greatest numbers in New Zealand. Newborn pups were seen on the Flinders Islands near Augusta in 1994, the first time the mammals were known to have bred there in 140 years. They were wiped out from most parts of Western Australia's south coast by sealers in the 1850s. The population is slowly recovering and about 70 fur seals now inhabit the Flinders group, up from the dozen or so usually seen there only a few years ago.

Sub-Antarctic fur seals and leopard seals, which have swum many thousands of kilometres from their breeding islands and principal feeding areas in the far south, are also occasional visitors to Western Australian waters.

Sea lions and fur seals can be recognised as "eared" seals by their earflaps. They differ from earless or "true" seals such as leopard seals, which have no external ear flaps and cannot use their hind legs when on land - they wriggle instead.

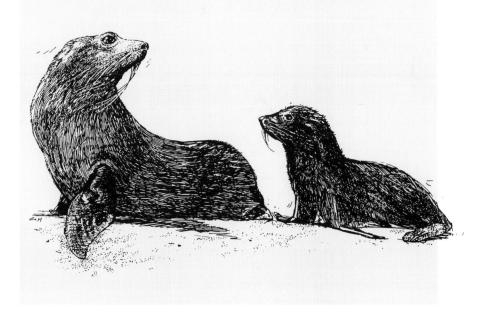

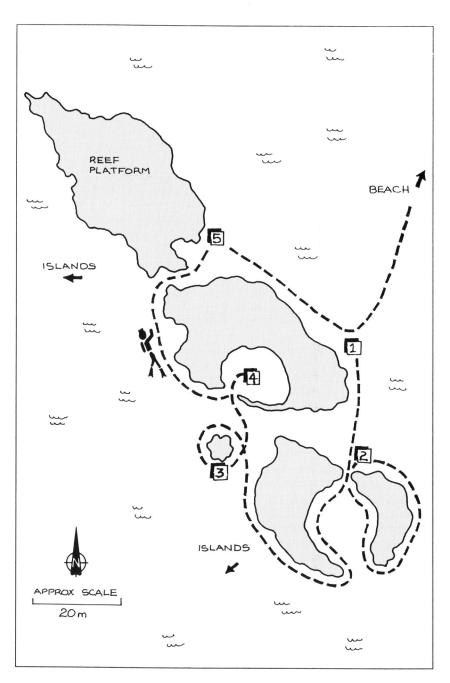

REEF
PLATFORM

ISLANDS

BEACH

5

1

4

2

3

ISLANDS

N

APPROX SCALE
20 m

Cosy Corner

How to get there: The turn-off to Cosy Corner is along Caves Road, 11 kilometres from the Bussell Highway.
Depth: 7 metres.

Because of its isolated position off the rugged coastline of the Leeuwin-Naturaliste National Park, this spot is still in pristine condition. Cosy Corner has a number of small islands surrounded by reef. The best way to dive the area is by taking a small boat from Hamelin Bay and anchoring on one of the sandy sheltered areas alongside the islands. Closer to the shore is the reef platform shown here. If you don't have a boat this is an excellent dive on either SCUBA or snorkel. However, the area can be hazardous and you should only dive it in the right conditions. Entry is from the beach and the reef is an easy swim from shore. The main problem is carrying heavy SCUBA equipment down the steep hill from the carpark. However, the effort will be well worth it. Because of the number of boats that use the area it is very important to advertise your presence with a dive flag.

1. Swim to the large reef platform not far from the beach. It is riddled with caves and overhangs along its edge. The caves are home to numerous fish species, especially scalyfin, western blue devils, red-lipped morwong and western foxfish. They are mostly curious and seem to have little fear of people. Cuttlefish, eagle rays and harlequin fish can also be seen lurking under ledges.
2. The section of reef platform furthermost from shore has a large hole carved in it by the sea and has separated in to two distinct sections. Swim through the gap and around the smaller section and then swim around the larger section of reef. You should see many species here including buffalo bream, black-headed puller, truncate coralfish, old wives, herring cale, white-barred boxfish, stripeys and zebra fish.
3. Circumnavigate the small lump on the seaward side of the reef platform.
4. Returning to the middle reef, you will notice another large round hole eroded by the ocean, then you can continue exploring the seaward side of the reef. Although species such as scalyfin are present in good numbers throughout the site, there is a different suite of species on the reef's more exposed side. You may see pike, zebra fish, bronze bullseye, skipjack trevally, goatfish, herring and banded sweep.
5. If you have time, explore another large lump close to the shore. Keep your eyes open for dusky morwong, samson fish, breaksea cod and many more. On your

return to the shore you may also be rewarded with interesting encounters. Bottlenose dolphins sometimes chase fish in the shallows. You could also see a brightly-coloured nudibranch, or sea slug, crawling along the sandy bottom, leaving a snail-like trail in the sand.

Caution areas: Swimming in to caverns and under ledges can be hazardous.
Degree of difficulty: Moderate.
Area's status: Cosy Corner is in the Leeuwin-Naturaliste National Park. It has been proposed that the waters should be considered for reservation as a marine park.

Carolyn Thomson and Peter Dans

CUTTLEFISH

Most people have memories of collecting cuttlebones washed on to the beach as children. These are the skeletons of the cuttlefish. The cuttlebone acts as a buoyancy mechanism for this animal, enabling the cuttlefish to remain on the bottom or swim freely at any depth. The density of the cuttlebone can be changed by pumping liquid in and out of chambers within it, thereby altering the volume of the gas-filled space.

Its means of movement is no less fascinating. Below the cuttlebone is a muscular mantle, which forms a cavity that is open at the front. When the mantle muscle contracts, this forces a jet of water through the funnel, strong enough to propel the animal through the water. Cuttlefish can also swim more slowly by moving their lateral fins. The water jet is also used to eject a cloud of ink if the cuttlefish is attacked, allowing it to escape. The original "India ink" was ink from cuttlefish collected in the Indian Ocean.

Cuttlefish have eight arms and two tentacles with which to capture food. They are usually retracted when not being used. The body of the common cuttlefish is about a foot long. It can disguise itself by changing colour, but usually has a zebra-like pattern.

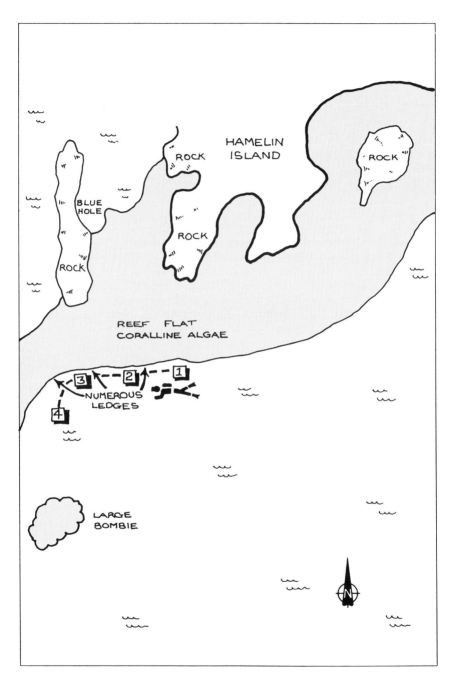

Hamelin Island

How to get there: *By boat from Hamelin Bay boat ramp.*
Depth: *9 metres.*

This dive basically follows the ledge along a section of the reef flat around Hamelin Island. It is a rewarding dive with numerous caverns, ledges and swimthroughs. It is also an area of great beauty. If conditions are suitable, there is also a large bombie offshore that would be well worth exploring (conditions prevented us from venturing there on our dive). A greater variety of marine life is found here than in inshore waters but there is obviously a greater degree of difficulty. Do not dive this site in north to north-westerly winds or when there is a heavy swell.

The platform reef that skirts Hamelin Island is partially exposed at low tide and awash at high tide. The reef flat adjacent to the dive site is a high energy environment washed with wave action and encrusted with sharp coralline algae. These areas support a great variety of marine organisms. Divers should avoid treading on them. They are not only very fragile and easily damaged but can also cause bad cuts.

1. Small is often very beautiful. Tiny blue-lined prettyfin form tiny splashes of iridescent blue. Another small fish - the black-headed puller - is just as colourful. They are yellow, black and silver.

2. There is a fantastic variety of fish species here. You may see schools of large buffalo bream, herring, striped seapike, old wives, schools of common bullseye, sea sweep and scalyfin. There are numerous western blue devils under ledges and in caves. The red-lipped morwong is unmistakable. It has red lips and brown to reddish-brown bands and spots on its head and body. Its colouration, however, allows it to camouflage itself easily in shaded ledges and caverns. Dusky morwong also inhabit these reefs.

3. At least one giant blue groper resides in the area. These fish grow to 1.6 metres and are a magnificent sight. Unfortunately, they are not often seen on WA's western coast due to fishing pressure. The aptly named harlequin fish have bright blue spots and yellow blotches on their sides. Blue-lined leatherjackets, horseshoe leatherjackets, juvenile mosaic leatherjackets, moonlighters, red-banded wrasse, maori wrasse and various species of boxfish also vie for attention.

4. Soft corals, gorgonians, sponges in a huge variety of forms and colours and sea squirts compete for space on every available surface. Sea fans, or gorgonian corals, are not reef-building corals. Despite their plant-like appearance, they are

animals. They usually grow at right angles to the current to catch plankton being carried past. Other animals include many varieties of starfish, and colourful nudibranchs.

Caution areas*: Swimming in to caverns and under ledges can be hazardous.*
Degree of difficulty*: Moderate.*
Area's status*: Hamelin Bay is in the Leeuwin-Naturaliste National Park. It has been proposed that the waters should be considered for reservation as a marine park.*

Carolyn Thomson and Andre Billstein with assistance from the Naturaliste Dive Centre

WHALE MIGRATION

Two species of whales can often be seen by boaters, or sightseers watching from vantage points on land, at certain times of the year - the humpback whale and the southern right whale.

Named because of the distinct "hump" that shows as the whale arches its back when it dives, the humpback is more coastal than most of the other large baleen whales. When in a playful mood, they may put on spectacular displays: breaching, rolling, finning and generally having a "whale" of a time.

Each year humpback whales migrate along the Western Australian coast, making their way between feeding grounds in the Antarctic and breeding areas on the North-West Shelf. Every year in early winter the herds move north and in spring and early summer they head south again.

Right whales are baleen whales, which feed on swarms of plankton, which they sieve from the water through the fibrous inner hairs of the baleen plates. During summer, right whales prefer the open ocean, away from the coast, but during late winter and spring the cows come in close to shore. There, near the surf line in sheltered bays, they give birth to their young, before returning to deeper waters as summer approaches.

The populations declined to dangerously low levels before whaling of these species ceased in 1959. Now, after nearly 30 years they are recovering and herds of humpbacks are once again becoming a spectacle as they pass through marine parks at Ningaloo, Shark Bay and Marmion. They can also be seen off the Leeuwin-Naturaliste coast.

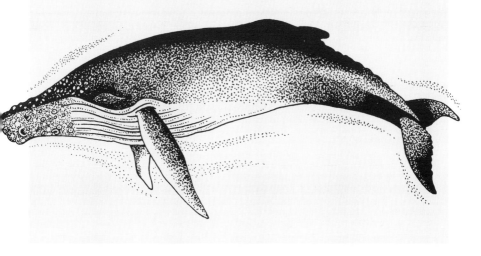

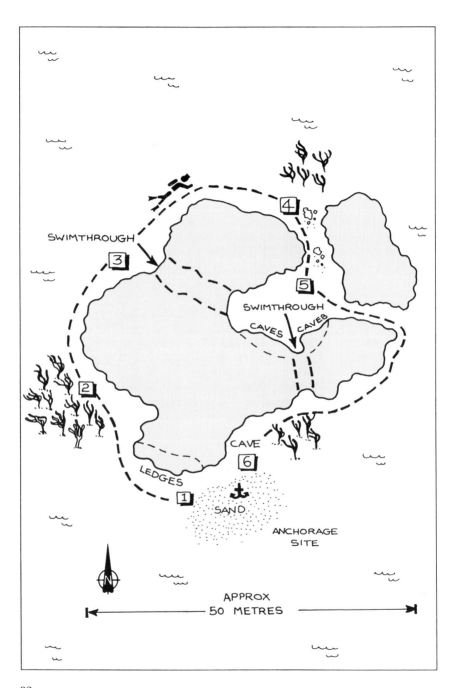

SWIMTHROUGH

3

4

5

SWIMTHROUGH

CAVES CAVES

2

CAVE

6

LEDGES

1

SAND

ANCHORAGE
SITE

N

APPROX
50 METRES

Bombie north-east of Hamelin Island

How to get there: By boat from Hamelin Bay boat ramp.
Depth: 9 metres.

These lumps lie a little to the north-east of Hamelin Island. They contain numerous caverns, ledges and swimthroughs packed in to a relatively small area. You may also be able to spot debris, possibly from a wreck. Because Hamelin Bay has so many hidden reefs and lumps, there are at least eight shipwrecks recorded in the area. Do not dive this site when winds are north to north-westerly or when there is a heavy swell.

1. Anchor in a patch of sand south of the lump. You will almost immediately see a reasonably deep ledge. The large variety of fish species found in and around the lumps includes herring, striped seapikes, buffalo bream, dusky morwong, rough bullseyes, common scalyfin, western scalyfin, black-headed pullers, blue-lined prettyfins, moonlighters, truncate coralfish, breaksea cod and banded sea perch.
2. Small fish such as senator wrasse play hide and seek amongst the dense kelp beds in the open areas around the lumps. Other wrasse species found here include slender wrasse and western king wrasse. Western foxfish are easily identified by the two yellow blotches that stand out on their orange to red bodies.
3. Continuing around the reef in a clockwise direction, you will come to a swimthrough. Port Jackson sharks live in this area. There are also many varieties of starfish.
4. There is an area of broken reef between the main reef and a smaller lump. Old wives may be seen fluttering together in schools, their delicate dorsal fins and black and white stripes providing a visual feast.
5. After swimming between the two reefs you will reach an open area surrounded by caves and swimthroughs. There are numerous western blue devils hiding under ledges and in these caves. Close investigation may also reveal cuttlefish and black stingrays in hidden nooks and crannies.
6. From here you can easily return to the anchorage site via further caves and swimthroughs and a nearby area of kelp. Among the numerous invertebrates you may see are gorgonians, soft corals and sponges, which grow in profusion on the roofs of caves and walls.

Caution areas: *Swimming in to caverns and under ledges can be hazardous.*
Degree of difficulty: *Moderate.*
Area's status: *Hamelin Bay is in the Leeuwin-Naturaliste National Park. It has been proposed that the waters should be considered for reservation as a marine park.*

Peter Lambert and Carolyn Thomson with assistance from the Naturaliste Dive Centre

SEA SQUIRTS

Sea squirts, or ascidians, derive their common names from the jet of water that is expelled from the body openings when these animals are compressed. They include sea tulips and colonial species that build large, complex colonies that coat the surface of underwater structures such as reefs, sea walls and jetties.

The animal begins life as a free-swimming tadpole with a rudimentary brain, eye spot and a primitive backbone. It soon attaches itself to a solid object and goes through an amazing transformation to become a kind of filtering sac that extracts oxygen and food from the sea water. Even the tiniest sea squirts may filter 170 litres of sea water each day. All sea squirts have two body openings - one to take in water and the other to expel wastes. They have a leathery or jelly-like covering of cellulose, known as a tunic, which may be translucent and may be brightly coloured.

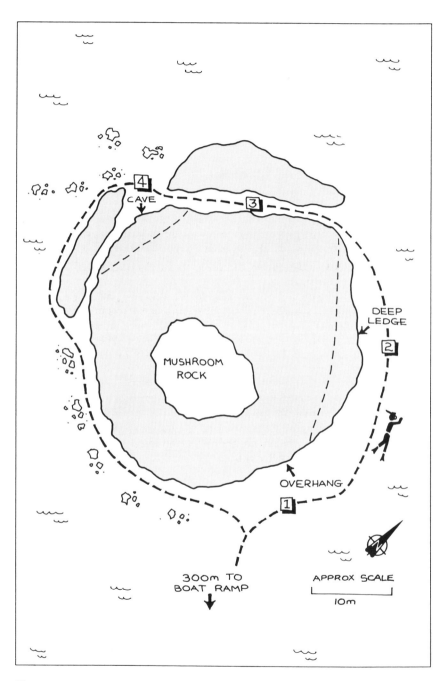

CAVE

MUSHROOM
ROCK

DEEP
LEDGE

OVERHANG

300m TO
BOAT RAMP

APPROX SCALE

10m

Mushroom Rock

How to get there: *Swim from shore or by small boat from Hamelin Bay boat ramp.*
Depth: *6-8 metres.*

Hamelin Bay offers excellent diving in a reasonably sheltered area. The Bay is full of reefs and shipwrecks. Divers can virtually take their pick from a huge range of sites. Of the four sites from Hamelin Bay mapped and described in this book, Mushroom Reef is the easiest to locate and reach. It is suitable for both SCUBA and snorkel diving. However, SCUBA diving is best done from a boat, as Mushroom Rock is a 300 metre swim from shore.

As you leave the boat ramp, you are likely to see at least one of the eagle rays or stingrays which inhabit the area. To your left you will see the remains of a 600 metre long jetty built in 1884. It was used to load ships with karri timber from Boranup Forest to be taken to markets throughout the world. At this time, the campsite at Hamelin was a timber yard and the nearby town of Karridale was the largest settlement in the area, housing more than 800 people. The last mill at Karridale closed in 1913.

1. Swim towards the prominent rock about 300 metres from shore. The reef around it is home to an abundance of marine life. There is a small overhang on the side of the reef nearest the jetty. The *Lovspring*, a 41 metre wooden-hulled Norwegian barque was wrecked on the Rock during a violent storm in July 1900. The vessel was smashed against the jetty and broke its mooring lines. Then it swung out from the jetty and was blown onto Mushroom Rock, where it sank. At daylight the crew were found clinging to the top of the cabin which was just above water level. However, the remains of the *Lovspring* have never been found.
2. Continue around the reef in an anti-clockwise direction, and find a deep ledge.
3. A channel between the main reef and a smaller reef just next to it is worth investigating. It is about six metres deep and crammed with marine life. The species list is impressive. It includes buffalo bream, dusky morwong, herring, zebra fish, old wives, senator wrasse, rough bullseyes, sea sweep, banded sweep, juvenile and adult scalyfin, black-headed pullers, red-lipped morwong, black-spotted wrasse and rough leatherjackets.
4. Just past this reef you will find another cave, on the main reef and adjacent to another smaller reef. Throughout the area you will see many varieties of starfish, cuttlefish and gorgonian corals.

Caution areas: *Swimming in to caverns and under ledges can be hazardous.*
Degree of difficulty: *Moderate - the dive is easy, but the swim is difficult.*
Area's status: *Hamelin Bay is in the Leeuwin-Naturaliste National Park. It has been proposed that the waters should be considered for reservation as a marine park.*

Andrew Horan and Glenn Wilmott with assistance from the Naturaliste Dive Centre

DRAGONS OF THE SEAS

What kind of fish looks like a cross between a seahorse and a piece of seaweed? A uniquely Australian creature - the leafy seadragon.

Seadragons are found only in southern Australian waters and hang almost motionless in the water, tiny fins fluttering to give stability and balance. Splashes of yellow, red and purple cover their bodies. They are slow swimmers, but their fragile, leafy appendages provide perfect camouflage in seagrass beds. Although quite common along our coast, they are rarely seen, even by experienced divers. Only the rolling of their eyes betrays them to predators.

Seadragons mate from September to December. The female produces 100 to 250 eggs, which she wipes against a wrinkled area of skin underneath the male's tail. The eggs stick to this patch, which forms cup-like moulds around the eggs. The oxygen-rich blood vessels in the tissue keep the egg supplied with oxygen during the eight-week incubation period.

A male seadragon caught by Underwater World had about 80 eggs, which were pink and covered in a green/brown algae. When they hatched, the young seadragons emerged tail first and swam freely after a few minutes. The yolk sac still attached to their bodies provided the young with two days' sustenance. After 50 days the young seadragons had grown 90 millimetres long. They took two years to reach their full size of 40 to 45 centimetres, and were then returned to the wild.

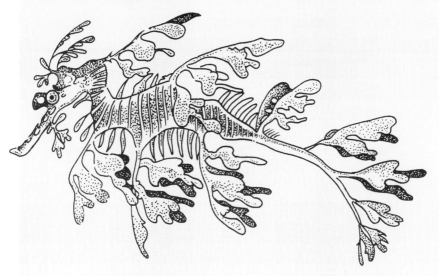

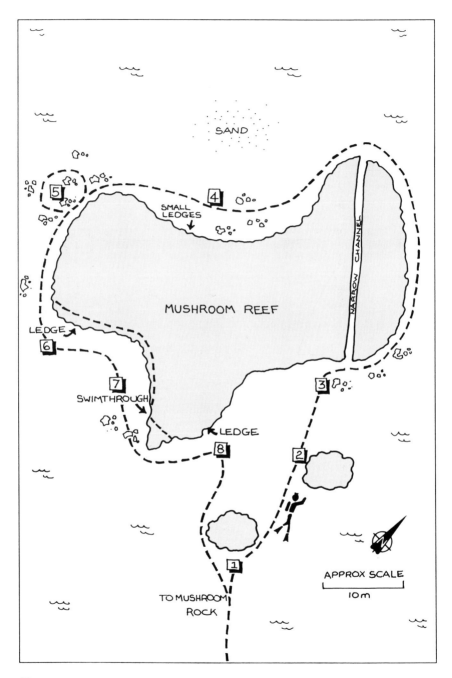

SAND

MUSHROOM REEF

NARROW CHANNEL

5

4

SMALL LEDGES

LEDGE

6

7

SWIMTHROUGH

3

LEDGE

8

2

1

TO MUSHROOM ROCK

APPROX SCALE

10 m

Mushroom Reef 6

How to get there: *Swim from shore or by small boat from Hamelin Bay boat ramp.*
Depth: *8 metres.*

Hamelin Bay has a colourful history. It was named after J Hamelin, one of many French explorers who visited WA between 1772 and 1817. Mushroom Reef, between Mushroom Rock and Peak Island, is suitable for both SCUBA and snorkel diving. SCUBA diving is best done from a boat, as the reef is a long swim from shore.

1. There is a small bombie between Mushroom Rock and the larger Mushroom Reef, where you may see a Port Jackson shark. They can be recognised by their attractive brown markings on a lighter body and fairly square head. Look for them in caves or adjacent patches of sand and weed. They have a spine behind their dorsal fins but are otherwise harmless.
2. Swim towards another bombie just to the north of the first.
3. Near an area of broken reef is a narrow channel that goes all the way through the reef. Fish species to look out for throughout the reef include buffalo bream, herring, zebra fish, old wives, senator wrasse, rough bullseyes, sea sweep, banded sweep, juvenile and adult scalyfin, black-headed pullers, red-lipped morwong, black-spotted wrasse and rough leatherjackets.
4. On the side of the reef nearest Peak Island is a patch of broken reef. There are also small ledges along the main reef to inspect.
5. Further around the reef is an area of broken reef, with many holes and ledges to explore. Look for beautiful gorgonian corals, starfish and cuttlefish.
6 & 7. Swim alongside a long, narrow ledge. As with most reefs in the area, elegant western blue devils lurk under ledges and in caves. As you head back to the starting point you may also locate a small swimthrough.
8. Before heading back to shore via the first bombie, there is another small ledge you may wish to find and investigate.

Caution areas: *Swimming in to caverns and under ledges can be hazardous.*
Degree of difficulty: *Moderate - the dive is easy, but the swim is difficult.*
Area's status: *Hamelin Bay is in the Leeuwin-Naturaliste National Park. The waters may become a marine park in the future.*

Andrew Horan and Glenn Wilmott with assistance from the Naturaliste Dive Centre

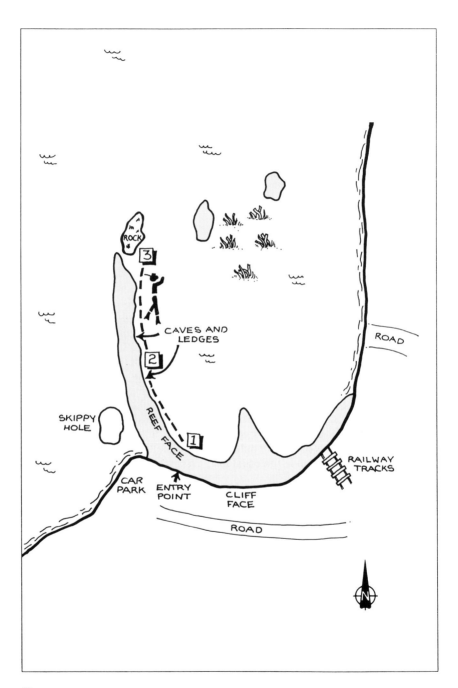

Kilcarnup

How to get there: Access to the beach is by a 4WD track off Caves Road.
Depth: Up to 6 metres.

The line of limestone reef that juts from the point has been eroded into some interesting caves and striking formations. The site is very protected and is home to some diverse and interesting marine life. With a depth of between four to six metres, it is a good site for snorkelling but it is also a worthwhile SCUBA dive. It is also an excellent night dive because the reef is well defined, so it is easy to navigate your way along it and back.

1. Because the reef is a fairly long and arduous swim from shore, it is suggested that you drive to the end of the point, from where you have only a 50 metre walk to the water's edge. It is, however, quite steep. Stay inside the line of reef that runs from the point, as conditions on the outer reef can be very rough. The reef has been spectacularly eroded, forming numerous caves and ledges.
2. Western blue devils hide in the many caves throughout the reef. Globe fish also inhabit the area. These comical-looking animals are related to blowfish. When they feel threatened, they swallow air until their entire body inflates and their yellow spines become erect. As well as having a fearsome appearance when inflated, their enlarged bodies would be quite difficult to swallow. Other reef fish found in the area include the usual old wives, scalyfin and various species of colourful wrasse.
3. Swim as far as the large rock that protrudes from the water further out in the bay, then return the same way. You will be sure to see schools of buffalo bream. In April, schools of salmon are running through the area. Other large fish include dusky morwong and blue groper.

Caution areas: Swimming in to caves and under ledges can be hazardous.
Degree of difficulty: Moderate.
Area's status: The beach and access road are part of a Shire reserve. The waters have been proposed as a marine park.

Carolyn Thomson and Andre Billstein

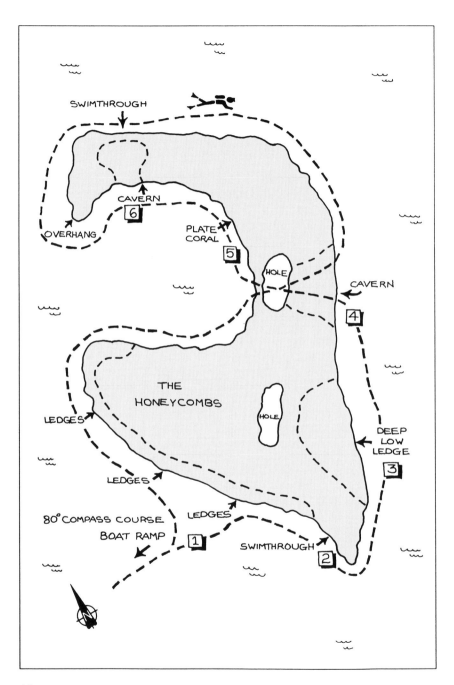

Canal Rocks - the Honeycombs

8

How to get there: *Park at Canal Rocks and swim 400 metres from the boat ramp.*
Depth: *6 metres.*

The fish species found in southern waters are often as colourful as any found on coral reefs. In fact, the diversity of marine plants and animals in southern Australia is amongst the highest in the temperate regions of the world. It is hardly surprising that the coastline from Vasse to Augusta has been proposed for reservation as a marine park.

Wait until the boat ramp is clear of boat traffic before entering the water. Stingrays and eagle rays are often seen around the boat ramp, where they scavenge for fish. Eagle rays can be distinguished by their very square heads, distinctively shaped wings and the blue to grey stripes on their backs. Swim from the boat ramp towards the point shown in the diagram below. It is about a 400 metre swim. You will know you are near the Honeycombs when you begin to see broken patches of limestone on the sea floor. If you hit a big sand patch you have gone too far.

Horizon viewed from the boat ramp

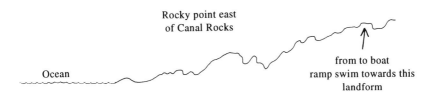

Rocky point east
of Canal Rocks

Ocean

from to boat
ramp swim towards this
landform

45

1. When you locate the Honeycombs, the long swim will be worthwhile. This is a heavily eroded limestone reef, with a great many caves, ledges and swimthroughs. The marine life is abundant. There are countless fish species at this site. There are also many starfish in a variety of shapes, sizes and colours.
2. Swimming around the reef in an anti-clockwise direction, you will encounter a small swimthrough.
3. Continuing around the reef you will notice a deep low ledge, under which several strikingly attractive western blue devils usually lurk.
4. A wide cavern with a hole at the back will take you to the other side of the reef. In and around this cave you may see old wives, senator wrasse, horseshoe leatherjackets, white-barred boxfish (distinctively shaped, with orange and white patterns on their bodies) and western foxfish. However, these are just some of the brightly-coloured fish that are easily identifiable.
5. Travelling clockwise now, you will notice an area of plate coral.
6. There is another cavern worthy of investigation. If you continue around the reef you will again find the large cavern described in point 4. If you swim through it you can return your starting point, inspecting the extensive ledges along the route, and thence return to the boat ramp.

Caution areas: Swimming in to caves and under ledges can be hazardous.
Degree of difficulty: Moderate - the dive is easy, but the swim is difficult.
Area's status: Canal Rocks is in the Leeuwin-Naturaliste National Park. It has been proposed that the waters should be considered for reservation as a marine park.

Carolyn Thomson, Duncan Melville and Mary Jo Hanley
with assistance from the Naturaliste Dive Centre

SEA CUCUMBERS

Sea cucumbers are sausage-shaped marine animals that are often seen concealing themselves in crevices, under stones or among seaweed, or burrowing in sand or mud. These dull-coloured beasts don't look particularly edible, but in some countries such as China some species of sea cucumbers (known as "trepang" or "beche-de-mer") found in the tropics are regarded as a delicacy.

The sea cucumber is an echinoderm, and is closely related to sea urchins and starfish. On the front of the body is a mouth surrounded by a ring of tentacles. Few would envy their lifestyle, but in their own way they are quite remarkable. They generally crawl across the sea bottom shovelling mud in to their mouths. After microscopic particles of food such as algae are extracted from the sediments, the remainder is excreted from the other end. The tentacles may also be used to capture tiny particles of food in the water.

When a sea cucumber becomes irritated, internal tubules attached to their respiratory organs fill with water. These are sticky and shoot out of the animal's anus, covering and distracting any predator. The sea cucumber can also eject the respiratory organ and gut. Remarkably, sea cucumbers can then regrow their missing parts.

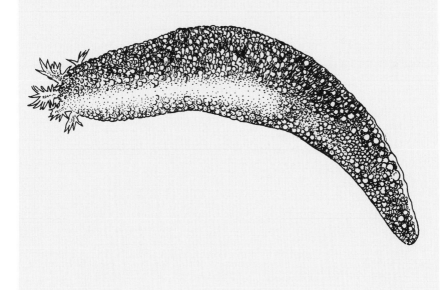

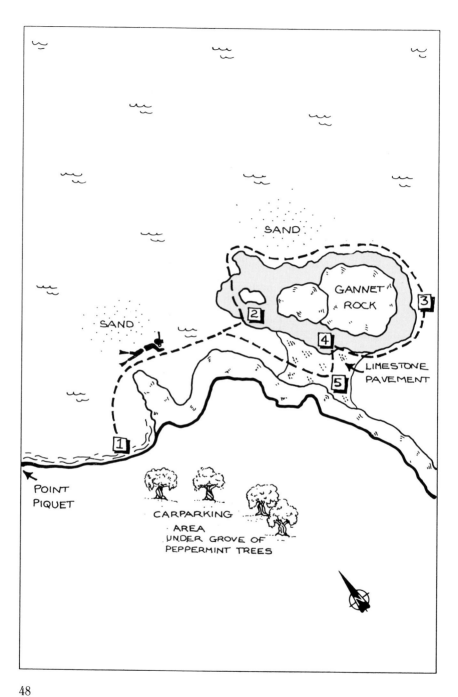

SAND

GANNET
ROCK

SAND

2

3

4

LIMESTONE
PAVEMENT

5

1

POINT
PIQUET

CARPARKING
AREA
UNDER GROVE OF
PEPPERMINT TREES

Gannet Rock

9

How to get there: *An unsealed track off the Eagle Bay-Meelup Road leads to a small parking area. The Rock is an 80 metre swim from shore.*
Depth: *3-4 metres.*

Gannet Rock is an enjoyable snorkelling site close to shore with diverse and interesting marine life. It is also an easy SCUBA dive, suitable for novices. It is protected in almost all weather conditions, with virtually no current. You may also see southern right whales in the shallows from August to November.

1. The best entry point is from the beach, from which Gannet Rock is an easy 80 metre swim. Give the anglers who often use the nearby rock a wide berth.
2. The part of the Rock nearest the beach has some interesting lumps and ledges. Old wives, supposedly named for their habit of "grunting like an old wife" when caught, are common. There are also many species of colourful wrasse and schooling fish such as herring and whiting.
3. This is an interesting area to explore ledges and lumps inhabited by samson fish, white-barred boxfish, wrasse, common scalyfin and many more fish species. Invertebrates include sea urchins, molluscs, sponges and cuttlefish. Cuttlefish feed on crabs, fish and other crustaceans. Like other close relatives such as octopus and squid, cuttlefish expel a cloud of ink when threatened. This provides a decoy so they can escape. Sea cucumbers can also be seen on the sea floor. These creatures ingest and then pass out large quantities of sand, removing the organic particles.
4. A swimthrough on the shoreward side of the Rock shelters a number of fish and invertebrate species. It is narrow and best examined from outside.
5. Between Gannet Rock and the mainland is a section of limestone pavement. A ledge along the rocks that fringe the mainland continues for some distance and is inhabited by dusky morwong and other fish. Dusky morwong are large, silvery-grey to bronze-grey and have large fleshy lips. They are common inhabitants of Western Australia's southern coastal waters.

Caution areas: *Swimming in to caverns and under ledges can be hazardous.*
Degree of difficulty: *Easy.*
Area's status: *Proposed marine park.*

Carolyn Thomson, Duncan Melville and Mary Jo Hanley

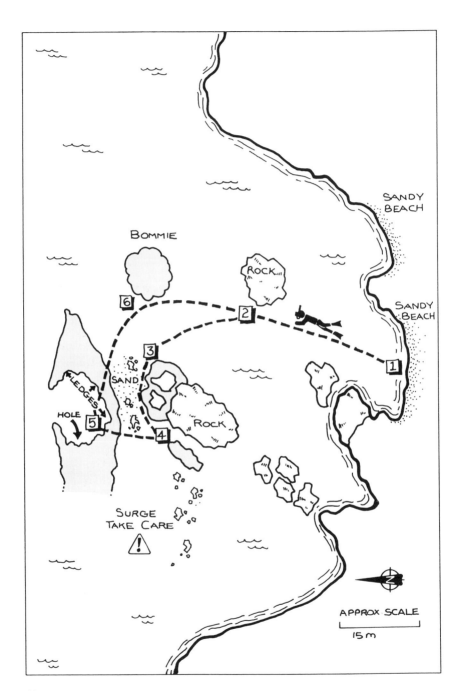

Bunker Bay - Shelley Beach

10

How to get there: Swim from Shelley Beach.
Depth: 5 metres.

Shelley Beach at Bunker Bay is a rewarding snorkelling site that is almost always protected. You will notice an unusual clicking sound all around you in the water. It is not known what causes this noise. The water here is also known for its yellowish tinge.

1. Entry is from a sandy beach. Swim towards the rock about 10 metres from shore.
2. There is little to see at the rock but you may spot buffalo bream, sweep and other fish species. Stingrays also inhabit the area.
3. The next point of interest is the large rock near the centre of the bay. The reefs and ledges around two big rocks which have separated from the main rock are interesting. Marine life includes red-lipped morwong, footballer sweep, prettyfins, garfish, moonlighters, stripeys (named because of their yellow and blackish stripes) and truncate coralfish. You will also see starfish of different shapes and sizes.
4. Swim around the rock to another reef, which is separated from the rock by a channel. This is also a good vantage point to look up and see the spectacular eroded cliff face overlooking the bay.
5. There is a hole about five metres deep with ledges around it, offering an interesting area for exploration. See if you can spot some brightly-coloured juvenile scalyfin. They progressively become more drab as they age. Boxfish and various colourful wrasse species can also be seen here.
6. On the way back you can inspect a bombie. You can either return to Shelley Beach and exit or swim around the headland and return to shore via a number of reefs elsewhere in Bunker Bay (see Bunker Bay - West Point on page 51).

Caution areas: Swimming in to caverns and under ledges can be hazardous.
Degree of difficulty: Easy.
Area's status: Bunker Bay is in the Leeuwin-Naturaliste National Park. The waters are proposed for reservation as a marine park.

Andre Billstein and Andrew Horan with assistance from the Naturaliste Dive Centre

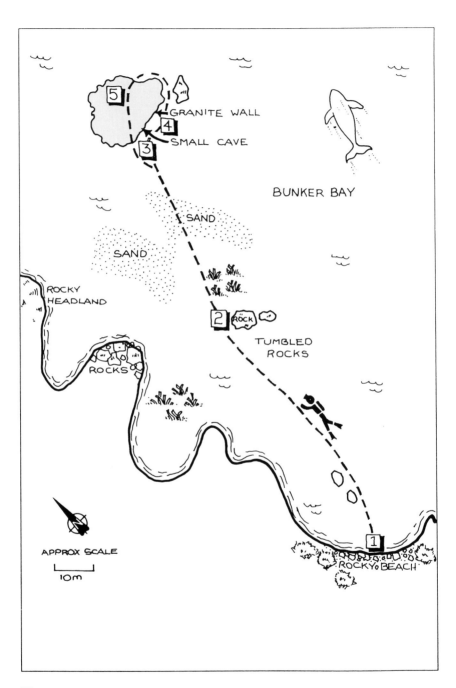

5

GRANITE WALL

4

SMALL CAVE

3

BUNKER BAY

SAND

SAND

ROCKY
HEADLAND

2 ROCK

TUMBLED
ROCKS

ROCKS

APPROX SCALE

10m

1

ROCKY BEACH

How to get there*: Swim from the beach just below Bunker Bay carpark.*
Depth*: 4-5 metres.*

Bunker Bay is suitable for both snorkelling and SCUBA diving and is reasonably sheltered in most weather conditions. However, like most dive sites in this area, you should not dive it if winds are north to north-west or if a moderate to heavy swell is running.

1. Entry is from the rocky beach below the carpark. Head towards the granite rocks about 30 metres from shore.
2. There is a broken rocky bottom of tumbled granites. The rocks are in shallow water only about three metres deep. Fish species include brown wrasse, slender wrasse, senator wrasse, scalyfin, roughies, Shaw's cowfish, bullseyes and schools of zebra fish. In the splash zone there are chitons and limpets, while whelks dwell in the weeds and rock on the bottom.
3. On the seaward side of the rocks there are seagrasses and algae, followed by a patch of sand. Head towards the bombies past the rocky headland to your left. The bombies are in about four and a half to five metres of water. Some interesting marine life shelters within a small cave with an overhang.
4. Swim in an anti-clockwise direction from the cave to encounter a sheer vertical granite wall, covered in a blaze of marine life. Pink, yellow and red sponges, soft corals, sea squirts and worms create a colourful display.
5. The lump almost breaks the surface in some places and drops away to three or four metres in others, creating a series of small shallow caves and ledges. You may swim over it to explore these nooks and crannies. Look for old wives, truncate coralfish, stripeys and buffalo bream. Starfish and sea cucumbers are also found in the area.

Caution areas*: Cobblers are found here so watch where you are treading.*
Degree of difficulty*: Easy.*
Area's status*: Bunker Bay is in the Leeuwin-Naturaliste National Park. The waters are proposed for reservation as a marine park.*

Peter Lambert and Glenn Wilmott with assistance from the Naturaliste Dive Centre

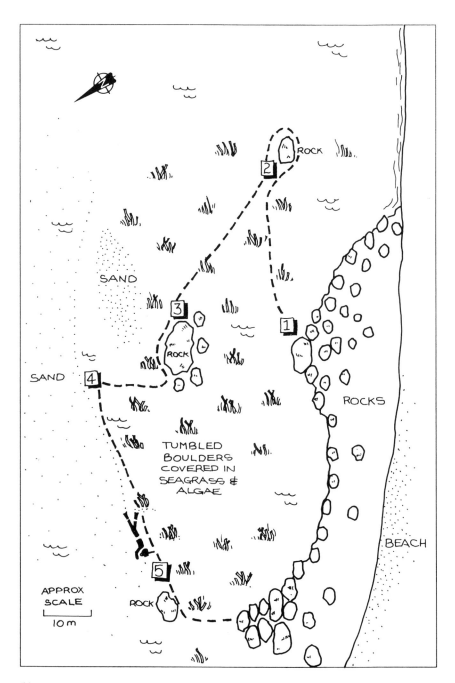

SAND

SAND

ROCK

ROCK

ROCK

ROCKS

BEACH

TUMBLED
BOULDERS
COVERED IN
SEAGRASS &
ALGAE

APPROX
SCALE
10m

2

3

1

4

5

54

Eagle Bay

How to get there: Park in the most northerly carpark at Eagle Bay and walk to the rocky area at the Bay's northern end.
Depth: 2-3 metres.

Although this area is very shallow, it is an idyllic spot. It is always very sheltered in the afternoons and the water is generally very clear. It is easy to reach and, while not the most challenging dive site, is recommended for snorkellers and is a good place to take the family. Here, the tumbled granite boulders on the beach continue out in to the Bay, where they have become overgrown with seagrasses and algae.

1. Entry is from the beach, beyond the rocks. Several fish species can be seen darting in and out of the seagrass and hiding in the many nooks and crannies under the granite rocks. They include moonlighters, zebra fish, blue-spotted goatfish, rough bullseyes, herring cale, herring, common scalyfin and gurnard perch. Iridescent blue and orange juvenile scalyfin are small but noticeable. Schools of tailor and tiny baitfish also frequent the area.

2. Swim to the small rock to the south and explore the marine life in and around it. Various molluscs, such as turban shells, are evident and starfish can be seen clinging to the granite rocks. They have hundreds of tiny suckers under their arms, enabling them to move around slowly. Most starfish are predators, using their arms to prise open the shells of their prey. They then turn their stomachs inside out through their mouths, to digest their victims.

3. A larger rock is another good spot for exploration. Senator wrasse and other wrasse species also inhabit the area. Wrasses are hermaphrodites and start life as females, but they have the ability to change into males, given the right stimulus. Upon the death of a male, the largest or most aggressive female goes through a metamorphosis to change into a larger, and usually more brightly coloured male fish.

4. About 40 metres from the shore, the seagrasses and algae end and a large sandy area begins. Along its perimeter, several fish can be seen darting in and out of the seagrass fronds. You may see rough leatherjackets. Leatherjackets have a single dorsal spine on their heads and are sandpapery to the touch. Most leatherjackets have a pointed snout and small mouth containing sharp teeth set in a strong jaw, which is useful for dismembering sea urchins and crushing small molluscs. They are active by day, but usually spend the night moored head-down in a bed of kelp or seagrass.

5. Another rock to the north is also worth an inspection before you make your way back to shore.

About 300-400 metres offshore there is a line of reef formed from the same granite rock seen on the shore. This reef, at depths of between five and 15 metres, offers a very rewarding dive. Ask at one of the local dive shops for directions, although you will need a small boat. Charters are available.

Degree of difficulty*: Easy.*
Area's status*: Proposed marine park.*

Carolyn Thomson and Glen Wilmott

Geographe Bay

Busselton Jetty

13

How to get there: *From shore or by boat (to dive the end structure). Charters operate several times a day (including night) during the busy summer period.* **Depth**: *7-8 metres.*

Busselton Jetty is the second longest wooden jetty in the southern hemisphere. It is a magnet for SCUBA divers. Although many invertebrates inhabit the piles close to the shore, the displays of coral and sponge are most spectacular at the end of the jetty. It is also an excellent night dive because it is almost impossible to get lost.

Thousands of invertebrates have built up around the piles, creating a bevy of colours and forms. Many are normally only found in deeper waters or under reef ledges, but exist here because the jetty protects them from the direct rays of the sun.

Piles near the end of the structure are covered with masses of telesto coral, which is coated with brilliantly-coloured sponges. During the day they look like colourful tree branches without leaves, but at night they display a profusion of brilliant white coral polyps, the density of which has to be seen to be believed. Amid this mass of waving fronds live hundreds of leatherjackets, boxfish, truncate coralfish, old wives, false Tasmanian blennies, black-throated threefins, globefish, clingfish and even unusual knight fish or pineapple fish. Gurnard perch cleverly disguise themselves as bits of wood, only their watchful eyes betraying them.

The molluscs include cowries, tritons and bivalves. Well-camouflaged octopuses shelter beneath fallen pylons, stray tentacles revealing their presence to observant divers. The most common nudibranch *Ceratosoma brevicaudatum* is seen on nearly every pile. The bright colours of these shell-less molluscs, or sea slugs, may serve as a warning to other species that they are poisonous or bad tasting.

The first 158.4 metres of the jetty was built in 1865, from giant karri hardwoods. It was used by whalers and other vessels. Further extensions were made in 1875, 1884, 1887, 1890, 1894, 1895 and 1896 as silt built up around the structure. It is now 1799 metres long but its future may be limited. Over the years the timber has been battered by storms and eaten away by marine worms and it is costly to maintain. Part of it may be demolished if it becomes a shipping hazard.

Caution areas: *Be wary of electric rays, blue-ringed octopuses, numbfish and gurnard perch. The jetty is a popular fishing spot so take care to avoid lines. Keep clear of boat traffic.*
Degree of difficulty: *Easy.*

Ann Storrie and Carolyn Thomson

PERTH AREA

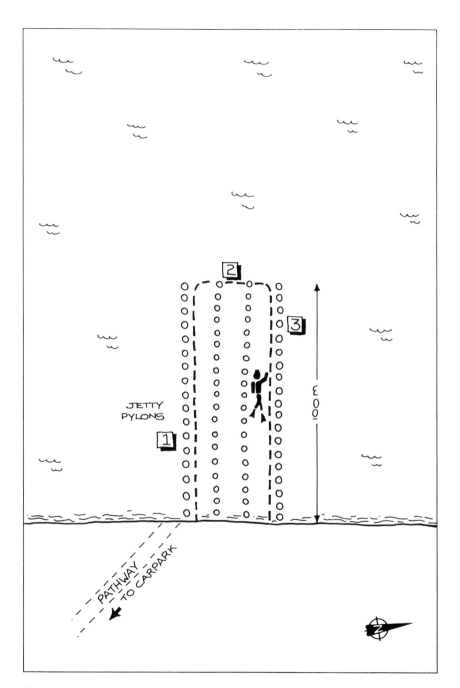

Woodman Point

14

How to get there: *Park at Woodman Point Recreation Area, off Cockburn Road.*
Depth: *7 metres.*

The jetty off the beach at Woodman Point, commonly called the "ammunitions" or "explosives" jetty, is about nine kilometres south of the mouth of the Swan River. The maximum depth is about seven metres.

1. The dive is short in length - only about 100 metres - but rich in colour and diversity. Examine the pier posts, which are covered with a great variety of invertebrate life. White, purple and pink sponges, feather duster worms, lacy stinging hydroids, a variety of anemones, sea stars, colourful nudibranchs, octopuses and other molluscs crowd on to each post, often draped with translucent veils of marine fungi.
2. At the end of the pier, the marine environment has reclaimed rejected logs and debris of an earlier era. Here, in the deeper water, the larger fish take advantage of the rich source of food. In turn, people on the pier try their hand at completing this particular food chain. Dangling fishing lines are a hazard.
3. Marine life is more diverse on the northern side of the jetty. You'll find a variety of fish feeding and sheltering amongst the invertebrates. Old wives, damselfish, leatherjackets, blennies, yellowtails and boxfish are all found in large numbers. Boxfish are easily identified by their unusual body shape and seemingly stunted fins. These quite slow-swimming animals occasionally squirt a jet of water in to the sand to uncover food such as invertebrates. A profusion of colourful sea stars and sand dollars litter the sand between the posts.

Caution areas: *Avoid fishing lines on either side of the jetty.*
Degree of difficulty: *Easy.*

Rae Burrows

Shoalwater Islands Marine Park

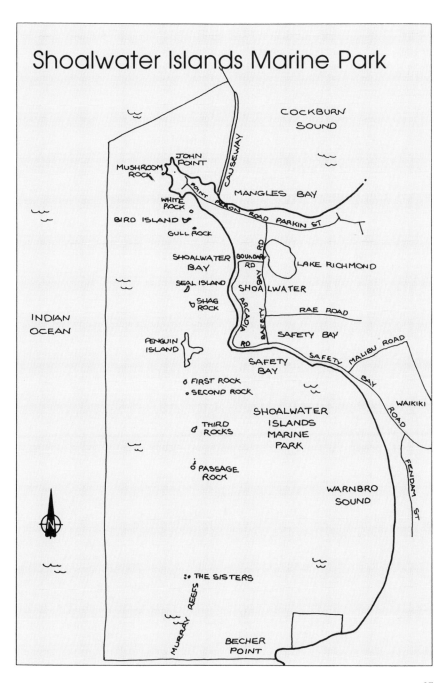

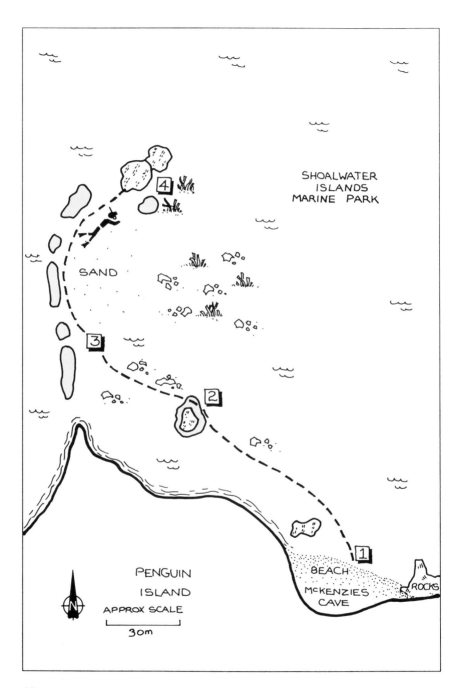

SHOALWATER
ISLANDS
MARINE PARK

SAND

PENGUIN
ISLAND

APPROX SCALE

30m

BEACH

McKENZIES
CAVE

ROCKS

North Penguin Island

15

How to get there*: By ferry from the mainland or by small boat.*
Depth*: 2-5 metres.*

This shallow and very sheltered area is packed with marine life. It is an ideal place to explore interesting underwater ledges and overhangs, lumps, low broken reef and seagrass areas. The trail can be dived in most weather conditions and there is no need to use SCUBA (which means you can stay in the water longer) or launch a boat. It is a very good area for beginners but more experienced divers will also find it fascinating. You can also incorporate an enjoyable ramble and picnic on Penguin Island into your excursion.

Penguin Island is the most northerly breeding site of the little penguin and an important breeding and resting area for many other seabirds such as bridled, crested and fairy terns. It is only a short ferry ride from the Shoalwater Visitor Centre at Mersey Point in Arcadia Drive, along Rockingham's Shoalwater Bay. You can reach the entry point by walking around the rocks along the north-eastern side of the island. Take extreme care if getting to this point by foot, and do not venture off the water's edge in to the seabird breeding areas. The underwater world around the island is protected by the marine park, so be careful to look but not touch.

1. There is a small sheltered beach near a collapsed cave, known to locals as McKenzies Cave. This is the starting point for the trail. Immediately off the beach is a reef platform that is overgrown with seagrass and algae. Beyond this is a sandy area and low broken reef. Head towards the small limestone rock about 30 metres from shore.

2. As you approach the rock, the broken reef becomes more prevalent. Just around it, there are interesting ledges and reefs inhabited by splash zone species such as chitons and snails. Have a good look around this area. There is a large seagrass patch to the east of the rock.

3. Swim in a westerly direction and you will locate a number of areas of upstanding reef platform. Follow these platforms, which have formed a gentle curve, towards a large rock on which birds such as cormorants often sit between their fishing forays. You will see various fish species, such as wrasse, and invertebrates, such as sponges and starfish, sheltering in the dense vegetation that has grown over the reefs. Take some time to investigate.

4. The rock is also surrounded by high broken reef to just below the surface - an interesting area for exploration.
5. You can either follow the same route back or swim directly back to the beach over the low broken reef, seagrass patches and sandy areas.

Caution areas: Swimming in to caverns and under ledges can be hazardous.
Degree of difficulty: Easy.
Area's status: The waters around the island are in the Shoalwater Islands Marine Park. Penguin Island itself is a conservation park.

John Edwards, Carolyn Thomson and Mike Cantelo

SEA LIONS

Western Australia is one of few places in the world where seals can be found relatively undisturbed on the doorstep of a major city. But have you ever wondered why there are no sea lion pups on the islands near Perth? It is because all sea lions that reside in the Perth metropolitan area are males. Every 18 months most of them leave the area and swim north to mate with the females that inhabit islands near Jurien and Cervantes (the species is the only sea lion in the world with an 18 month breeding cycle). After the breeding season they return to Seal Island, Carnac Island and their other favourite resting areas around Perth. This migration is thought to take the feeding pressure off the females and young pups in the northern breeding areas.

Sea lion numbers were greatly reduced by sealers in the eighteenth and nineteenth centuries. Now the Australian sea lion is the rarest in the world and the species is given special protection under State legislation. Australian sea lions breed and rest on offshore islands from the Abrolhos, near Geraldton, to Pages Island, just east of Kangaroo Island in South Australia. The species is the only seal or sea lion that is unique to Australian waters.

If you are diving near seals or sea lions, you should never approach them. Allow them to approach you if they wish. Never attempt to touch a seal. Keep your hands close to your body and your movements to a minimum, to avoid startling the animal. If a seal becomes overly playful or aggressive (such as nipping at flippers or nudging your body) you should move away cautiously and leave the water.

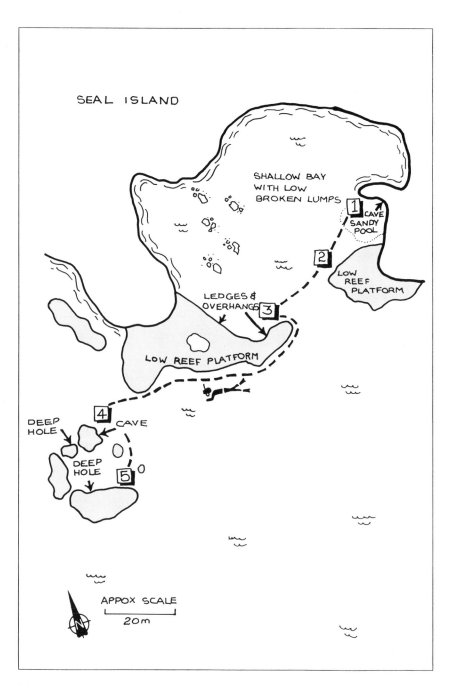

SEAL ISLAND

SHALLOW BAY WITH LOW BROKEN LUMPS

1 CAVE
SANDY POOL

2

LOW REEF PLATFORM

LEDGES & OVERHANGS

3

LOW REEF PLATFORM

DEEP HOLE

4 CAVE

DEEP HOLE

5

APPOX SCALE
20m

N

South end of Seal Island

16

How to get there: By boat from Safety Bay.
Depth: 1-5 metres.

This is a safe and enjoyable trail, suitable for young snorkellers and family groups. The trail, within a sheltered bay on the south side of Seal Island, is protected in most weather conditions. There is also much for experienced snorkellers to enjoy, especially the chance to see sea lions relaxing in the wild *en route* to the dive.

As you approach the eastern side of Seal Island, you will see a number of large chocolate brown shapes on the beach. A colony of Australian sea lions hauls out on the island for most of the year. Although they are one of our most attractive and interesting sea creatures, sea lions can deliver a nasty bite if aggravated. They are curious and may approach your boat. To avoid disturbing the animals, which are territorial, you are asked not to land on the island. Instead, anchor on the west side of the island.

1. A cave found on the eastern side of the bay is a delightful place to explore. Within it is a shallow pool filled with old turban shells and other debris. Growing over the shells and rocks, you can see pink encrusting coralline algae and other interesting life forms, including small yellow sponges. Sponges feed by filtering sea water through their bodies to extract tiny living creatures or microscopic specks of organic matter. They obtain oxygen in the same way.
2 & 3. Low reef platforms enclose the outer edges of the bay. The reef platform on the western side contains many interesting ledges and overhangs. Look for colourful soft corals and small fish that dart out of the many holes.
4. While the youngsters are exploring the sheltered bay, you can inspect some interesting lumps further out (but well within swimming distance). In the first is a deep hole that is inhabited by fairly large fish such as buffalo bream.
5. A little further out is an upstanding reef platform with many sheer faces.

Caution areas: Swimming in to caverns and under ledges can be hazardous.
Degree of difficulty: Easy.
Area's status: Lies within the Shoalwater Islands Marine Park. Seal Island is a nature reserve.

John Edwards, Carolyn Thomson and Mike Cantelo

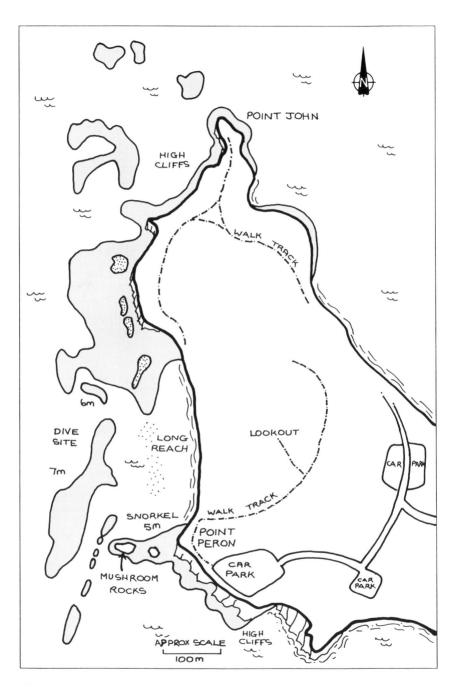

POINT JOHN

HIGH CLIFFS

WALK TRACK

DIVE SITE

6m

7m

LONG REACH

LOOKOUT

SNORKEL 5m

WALK TRACK

POINT PERON

MUSHROOM ROCKS

CAR PARK

CAR PARK

CAR PARK

APPROX SCALE

100m

HIGH CLIFFS

Cape Peron

17

How to get there: *Enter the water from the beach at Long Reach.*
Depth: *3-7 metres.*

Cape Peron is one of the best shore dive or snorkelling sites in the Perth metropolitan area. The waters surrounding the limestone headland are dotted with numerous reefs, caves and swimthroughs. You can reach the best diving and snorkelling sites from the beach at Long Reach. The north and south ends of this beach are gently sloping and sandy, allowing easy entry. In the centre is a flat beach rock platform that drops to about 1.5 metres of water.

Sea urchins and sea anemones shelter in the seagrasses near shore. The species of sea urchin that is commonly found here has a habit of attaching bits of shell to itself at low tide, possibly to protect itself from the sun. Other inhabitants of the shallow sandy areas include turban shells, plump sea stars, spider crabs and anemones. As you swim out to the fringing reef, you will notice fish such as whiting and baitfish congregating in schools. Baitfish are an important part of the diet of Penguin Island's little penguins.

Point Peron and Mushroom Rocks are ideal snorkelling sites. The limestone has been carved into numerous overhangs, small caves and swimthroughs very close to shore in a maximum depth of five metres. They protect a quieter world of different invertebrates and fish. Colourful encrusting sponges, sea squirts, feather stars, lacy bryozoans and hard corals can be found clinging to the limestone.

The reefs about 150 metres from the north and south end of Long Reach beach are ideally suited to SCUBA diving. The underwater features lie in water up to seven metres deep. Here, the swimthroughs are bigger and the caves deeper. Old wives, various wrasse and red-lipped morwong are relatively common.

An alternative entry site is the beach just west of the Ministry of Sport and Recreation camp school. This entry provides good access to the Point John reef.

Caution areas: *Care should always be taken in caverns and under ledges.*
Cobblers shelter in the seagrass beds.
Degree of difficulty: *Easy.*
Area's status: *Shoalwater Islands Marine Park.*

Peter Dans and Rae Burrows

Carnac Island

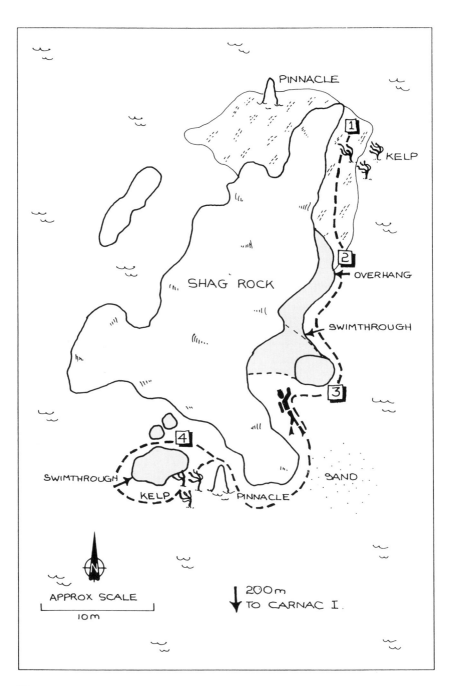

PINNACLE

1

KELP

2

OVERHANG

SWIMTHROUGH

3

4

SWIMTHROUGH

KELP

PINNACLE

SHAG ROCK

SAND

N

APPROX SCALE

10m

200m

TO CARNAC I.

Carnac Island - Shag Rock

18

How to get there: *By boat from Fremantle (6 nautical miles) or elsewhere.*
Depth: *4-8 metres.*

Shag Rock is easily found. This large rock is north of Carnac Island (north of Currie Point and east of Fraser Point). This is a good dive, with a great many overhangs and swimthroughs. The invertebrate life is similar to that seen in the Marmion Marine Park. However, it is recommended that novice divers and snorkellers stay on the east side, which is more sheltered. There is less to see on the west side and it is subject to strong surge.

1. The north part of Shag Rock has an interesting assemblage of limestone pinnacles, limestone pavement and rubble, in which turban shells and other molluscs can be seen. There are also patches of kelp. Fish species include buffalo bream, banded sweep and various species of wrasse. Buffalo bream differ from most other south-western fish in that they feed primarily on algae.
2. On the eastern side there are many overhangs, with diverse invertebrate life such as gorgonian and other soft corals, sponges in numerous colours and ascidians (sea squirts). Many sea urchins can be seen in the kelp and rubble. *Posidonia* seagrass, recognised by its ribbon-like leaves, can also be seen growing in this area, along with kelp and sea lettuce. *Posidonia sinuosa* and *Posidonia australis* often grow together in mixed beds. They are the most common seagrass species around Perth, but another 16 plants also grow in the region. Animals such as snails, crustaceans and worms move up and down the seagrass blades in search of food. A large proportion of these creatures feed on the filamentous seaweeds attached to the seagrass leaves or on the smaller animals. Very few are capable of eating and digesting the cellulose-rich seagrass itself.
3. Part of the reef lies in the intertidal zone, and displays typical communities of barnacles, molluscs, and other shellfish. The fringing reef platform is carpeted with delicate coralline algae formations which are easily destroyed by walking on the reef.
4. The south end of the rock is less sheltered but offers an interesting and enjoyable area for exploration. There are a number of excellent swimthroughs and overhangs amid several lumps.

Degree of difficulty*: Moderate.*
Area's status*: Nearby Carnac Island is a nature reserve managed by the Department of Conservation and Land Management. The waters surrounding the island have been proposed for consideration as a marine park.*

Dave Burton and Peter Dans

SEA URCHINS

Heart urchins, cake urchins and sand dollars are just some of the many species of sea urchins. So are some tropical species with venom-tipped spines that can cause severe pain to careless divers. These unusual animals provide an endless source of fascination.

Sea urchins are most common in intertidal habitats and on shallow reefs, but have been found as deep as 7000 metres. They are closely related to starfish, sharing the same five-fold symmetry, and they too move about on hundreds of hydraulically-operated tube feet. Starfish and sea urchins are from a group known as echinoderms, a word meaning "spiny skins". Sea urchin spines protect them from predators. Some species also use the spines on the underside to move around, making them look like they are walking on stilts. They feed on kelp and other forms of algae. Due to their ability to reproduce rapidly when conditions become favourable, they can reach plague proportions and have a devastating effect on certain marine environments. People are one of their main predators. In some parts of the world sea urchins are believed to be powerful aphrodisiacs. The roe is a prized delicacy in Japan, in islands of the Pacific and in European countries such as France, Italy and Greece.

Sea urchin eggs have properties that make them important for medical research. Compounds extracted from marine organisms are initially tested to see whether they inhibit the production of rapidly dividing sea urchin eggs. If so, they may have potential to provide cures for AIDS, cancer and other diseases.

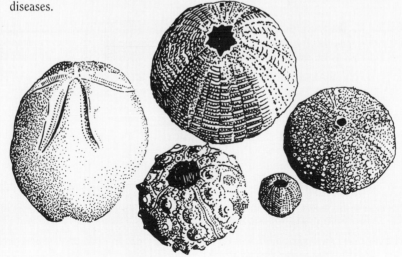

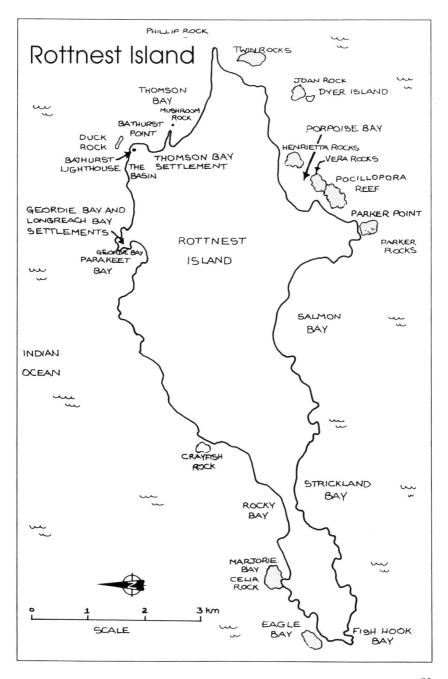

Rottnest Island

PHILLIP ROCK

TWIN ROCKS

JOAN ROCK
DYER ISLAND

THOMSON BAY
MUSHROOM ROCK

BATHURST POINT

DUCK ROCK

PORPOISE BAY

HENRIETTA ROCKS
VERA ROCKS

BATHURST LIGHTHOUSE

THOMSON BAY SETTLEMENT

THE BASIN

POCILLOPORA REEF

GEORDIE BAY AND LONGREACH BAY SETTLEMENTS

PARKER POINT

PARKER ROCKS

ROTTNEST ISLAND

GEORDIE BAY
PARAKEET BAY

SALMON BAY

INDIAN OCEAN

CRAYFISH ROCK

STRICKLAND BAY

ROCKY BAY

MARJORIE BAY
CELIA ROCK

0   1   2   3 km

SCALE

EAGLE BAY

FISH HOOK BAY

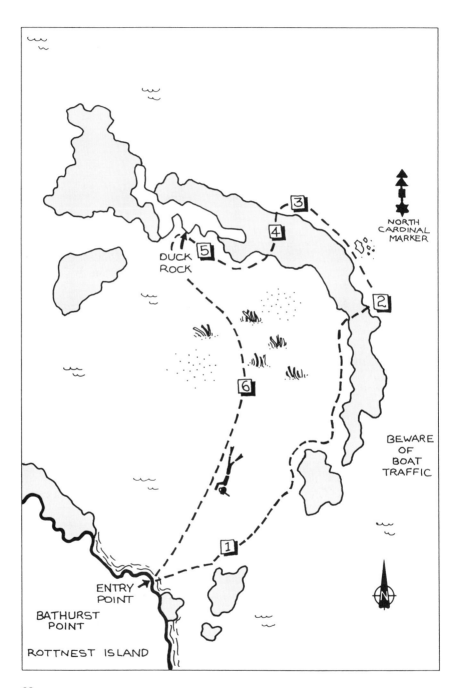

NORTH
CARDINAL
MARKER

3

4

5

DUCK
ROCK

2

6

BEWARE
OF
BOAT
TRAFFIC

N

1

ENTRY
POINT

BATHURST
POINT

ROTTNEST ISLAND

Duck Rock

19

How to get there: *Swim from Bathurst Point.*
Depth: *Up to 6 metres.*

Duck Rock is a fun and interesting diving or snorkelling site that is accessible from shore. It is also an easy walk from the settlement at Thomson Bay. The reef flat around the Rock is riddled with some medium-sized caves, ledges and swimthroughs. You may even see some wreck remains. The maritime history of Rottnest dates back to the seventeenth century and the remains of 14 wrecks lie around the Island.

1. Enter the water from Bathurst Point and follow the line of reef to Duck Rock. Stay on the side of the reef nearest the shore to avoid any conflict with boat traffic.
2. Locate some wooden timber that may have originated from the wreck of the *Transit*. The 124-tonne two-masted schooner was wrecked in 1842, after striking Duck Rock on a voyage between Bunbury and Fremantle. The cabin rapidly filled with water and the captain saved only his chronometer and his desk containing 120 gold sovereigns.
3. The north-eastern side of the rock is the best area for snorkelling, so spend some time here exploring the caverns, swimthroughs and holes. Reef fish shelter in the many nooks and crannies, including numerous scalyfin (especially tiny brightly-coloured juveniles), western foxfish, red-lipped morwong and wrasse of various kinds. Schools of buffalo bream are common.
4. On top of the reef flat you will notice small colonies of pink pocillopora coral, which can be seen growing extensively at Pocillopora Reef at Parker Point.
5. Swim along the southern side of the rock. There is less marine life to see here, but you may be rewarded with some interesting sightings.
6. Return to shore via an area of seagrass and sand. Keep an eye open for stingrays, King George whiting and dusky morwong.

Caution areas: *Take care to avoid passing boats and always use a dive flag.*
Degree of difficulty: *Moderate.*
Area's status: *The waters around Rottnest are a marine reserve. Wrecks are protected by law and no artefacts can be removed or damaged.*

Carolyn Thomson, Peter Dans and Kevin Crane

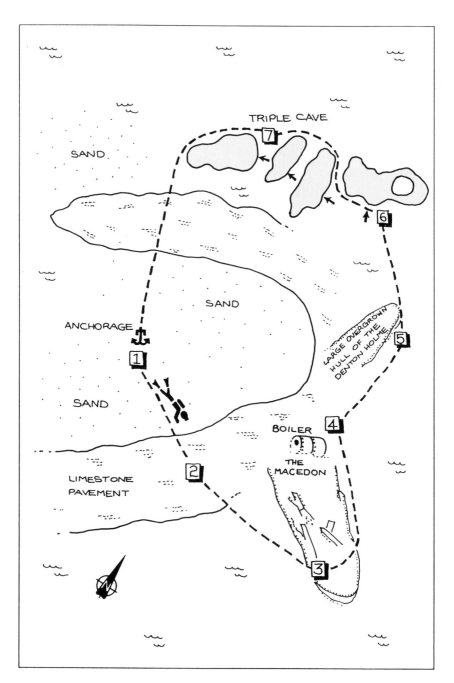

TRIPLE CAVE

SAND

SAND

ANCHORAGE

SAND

LIMESTONE
PAVEMENT

BOILER

THE
MACEDON

LARGE OVERGROWN
HULL OF THE
DENTON HOLME

1

2

3

4

5

6

7

West Kingston Reef 20

How to get there: By boat.
Depth: Up to 7 metres.
Coordinates: The Macedon *is at latitiude 31°59'16" south, longitude 115°33'20"* east. The Denton Holme *is at latitude 31°59'14" south, longitude 115°33'19"* east.

West Kingston Reef (Transit Caves) is one of the most interesting around Rottnest Island and also features the wrecks of the *Macedon* and *Denton Holme*. Moor on the courtesy mooring or, if it is occupied, in the sandy area west of the wrecks. This is a very good dive when conditions are calm or during south-westerly winds, usually in summer. Be sure, however, to take enormous care when locating the site, as there are submerged reefs and wreck remains throughout the area. The wrecks are accurately marked on the Rottnest Island chart.

1. To avoid damaging fragile reefs, anchor in the sandy patch indicated. Keep an eye open for rays camouflaged on the sandy bottom.
2. Swim south from the mooring area until you reach an area of limestone pavement. Invertebrate life on this broken reef includes a proliferation of sea urchins.
3. The wreck of the *Macedon*, an iron steamer which sank on the reef in 1883, is the most intact of the two wrecks. Juvenile blue groper, which are a greyish-brown colour rather than the dark blue of the adults, may be seen. This species is quite spectacular when fully grown but is uncommon on the western coast of Western Australia due to fishing pressure. Fortunately, Rottnest Island is a marine reserve and spearguns cannot be used in the area.
4. You can clearly see the boiler and the hull of the wreck, which you can use to orientate yourself. The ship had 50 passengers, including future premier John Forrest and surveyor Alexander Forrest, and 40 horses aboard. All were safely rescued.
5. To the north of the boiler is the second wreck, a large flattened hull, around 45 metres long. The *Denton Holme*, a 998-tonne iron sailing ship, was wrecked in 1890. It was on a voyage from Glasgow carrying 1275 tonnes of water pipes, as well as general cargo. The remains are overgrown and hard to discern.
6. Further north is a series of four spectacular, high-reef caves crammed with fish and invertebrate life. The wreck of the *Janet* also lies on these caves. Although it is broken up, you may see some remains. The underwater landscape around

Rottnest is a drawcard for divers, because its proximity to deeper water brings a wealth of marine life and because the limestone that also forms the island itself has eroded to form spectacular cave formations, swimthroughs and grottos. You can examine a limestone grotto within the first lump.

7. Explore a series of three caves in three adjacent lumps. Fish life in this area includes King George whiting, various species of leatherjacket and wrasse, in fact any of the reef and oceanic species. King George whiting can be distinguished by the many small brown spots on their fairly elongated bodies. Leatherjackets feed mostly on bottom-dwelling invertebrates. Australia has more species of leatherjackets than any other region, and they are found mostly in temperate and sub-tropical waters. You will see a variety of plate and soft corals. Sponges are plentiful and are found in a great variety of shapes and colours.

Caution areas: Be wary of submerged reefs and remains of the wrecks, which are close to the surface in places. Swimming in to caverns and under ledges can be hazardous.
Degree of difficulty: *Moderate.*
Area's status: The waters around Rottnest Island are a marine reserve. West Kingston is also a protected wreck site and artefacts can't be removed from the area.

Greg Pobar

THE LEEUWIN CURRENT

In autumn and winter a fascinating phenomenon takes place along the Western Australian coast that has far-reaching consequences for the distribution of marine life throughout the area. The Leeuwin Current is a band of warm, low-salinity water that moves south from Exmouth to Cape Leeuwin. On reaching Cape Leeuwin, it flows eastward to Esperance.

In winter, when it is at its strongest, the Leeuwin Current can usually be identified from satellite imagery as a stream of warm water moving down the upper continental slope. It is around 50 kilometres wide and 200 metres deep and moves south at a rate of between one and three knots. It appears to originate as a result of a complex pattern of water circulation from the Western Pacific Ocean through the Indonesian Archipelago and from currents and eddies in the Indian Ocean.

The current transports larvae of tropical marine life, such as corals, south and provides a flow of warmer water that enables many tropical and sub-tropical species to survive further south than they would in other parts of the world. The many tropical fish that proliferate in Perth's Marmion Marine Park and on the spectacular reefs around Rottnest Island can also be attributed to the Leeuwin Current.

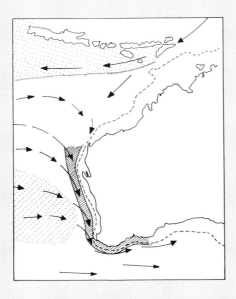

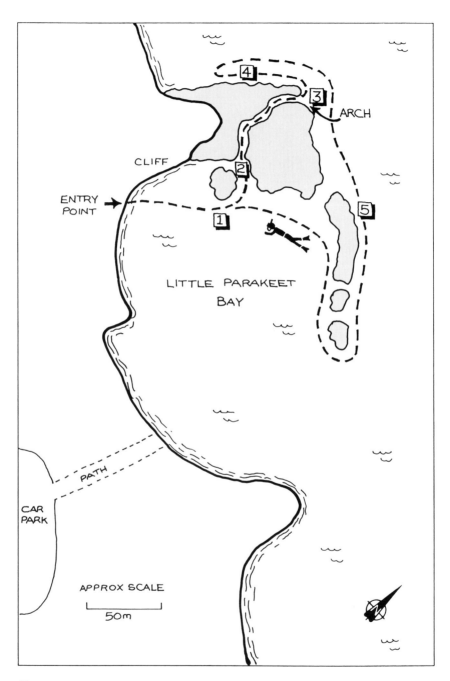

ARCH

CLIFF

ENTRY
POINT

LITTLE PARAKEET
BAY

PATH

CAR
PARK

APPROX SCALE

50m

Little Parakeet Bay

21

How to get there: *Catch a bus, ride your bike or walk to Little Parakeet Bay. It is less than a kilometre north-west of Geordie Bay. Enter the water at the western end of the bay.*
Depth: *1-4 metres.*

Little Parakeet Bay is a small sandy bay encircled by craggy cliffs and limestone reefs. It is a morning dive or snorkel site, located on the northern side of Rottnest Island, so it is well protected from the south-easterly winds.

1. Enter the water at the western end of the bay, about a 300 metre walk from the carpark, and swim out to a small bombie.
2. Just adjacent to the bombie there is a narrow chasm in the reef platform that you can follow. It is only about a metre wide and can just fit a person through it. The kelp which grows thickly on the sides of this channel hides a wonderland of colour, including brilliant orange and blue nudibranchs, and tubby vivid red starfish. Take some time to seek these and other treasures amongst the mini-forest of kelp.
3. The channel will bring you to a wider opening in the reef and an underwater arch. The movement of water in and around this area, combined with the amount of sunlight streaming through the wider opening in the reef makes for a greater variety of plants and animals. You can either hang above the tabloid and watch, or fin down for a closer look. Under the arch there are sea squirts, encrusting sponges and corals. There are sea urchins which have used their spines to dig themselves firmly in to the limestone, and there are fish lurking or sprinting everywhere.
4. Follow the reef line to the left after you leave the arch. On your right are seagrass beds, and on your left are ledges under the reef platform. The seagrass in this area is mainly *Amphibolus*. There are numerous bald patches where you'll be able to watch the beautiful marine worms. Housed in tubes of calcium carbonate, the feathery tentacles of these creatures filter food from passing currents. The tentacles are retracted in to the tube when the animal is disturbed. Keep a sharp eye out for stingrays in the sandy area as well. They are masters of concealment and are rarely seen by novice snorkellers, but are well worth observing. Watch for the lazy juvenile Port Jackson sharks which rest on the ledges of the reefs. They are only about 30 centimetres long and are generally reluctant to leave their comfortable resting places.

5. Fin back to the arch and follow the reef around the bay. You are bound to find more marine wonders.

Caution areas: *Well protected except during times of strong westerly winds. Take care that equipment does not damage reef organisms, particularly in narrow channels and arches.*
Degree of difficulty: *Easy.*
Area's status: *The waters around Rottnest are a marine reserve.*

Rae Burrows and Greg Pobar

STARFISH

These fascinating marine animals consist of a central disc and five or more radiating arms. At the tip of each arm is a small red eye and beneath the body is a central mouth. Turn one over and you can see its tube feet, each with a suction disc at the tip, which it uses to move about. Starfish are found in a great variety of sizes, forms and colours. They are usually red, orange, pink or yellow but grey, green, blue or purple ones can also be seen.

Starfish are remarkable in being able to regenerate lost or damaged parts of their bodies. An arm that is broken off can be regrown. Some species can actually regrow a complete new body from a single severed arm, if it is attached to part of the central disc.

Most starfish devour shellfish, but some eat sea urchins, sea cucumbers and other starfish. They feed by extruding their stomach over corals or between the shells of bivalves. A few catch small fish or shrimps with pincers on the top of their bodies, then pass the animals around to their mouths by using their tube feet.

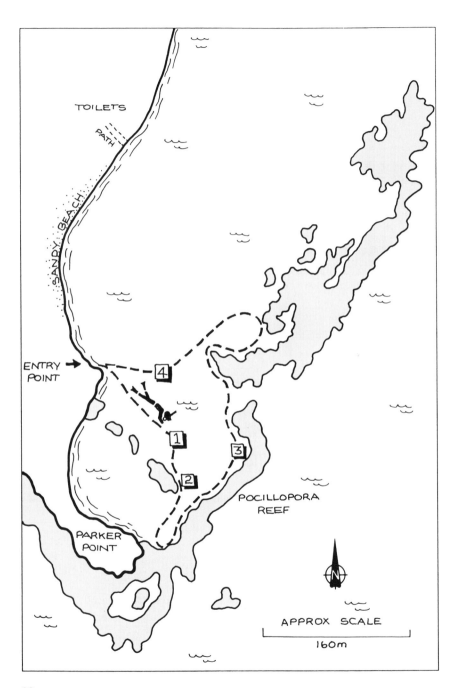

TOILETS

PATH

SANDY BEACH

ENTRY POINT

4

1

2

3

POCILLOPORA REEF

PARKER POINT

N

APPROX SCALE

160m

Pocillopora Reef - Parker Point

22

How to get there: Take a boat or swim from the shore.
Depth: 1-3 metres.

The reef is named after the species of beautiful pink coral *Pocillopora damicornis* that grows there in profusion. The coral reef community is completely different to any you will see anywhere else in Perth and the variety of fish and invertebrate life is astounding for such a small area. The reef is easy to reach from shore and easy to see on snorkel, so very minimal effort is required to complete a magnificent dive. You can virtually dive on a tropical coral reef without leaving Perth. Walk south along the sandy beach until you reach the rocky point at the end. This is your entry point.

1. Swim towards the reef near the point, where you will come across clumps of pink coral. The clumps are initially sparse and interspersed with sand and seagrass patches. The formations of coral are extremely delicate and you should take care not to touch or accidentally kick them. Each community was formed from a single individual polyp that cloned and budded off innumerable times, creating a colony of thousands of genetically identical individuals. Dusky morwong, red-lipped morwong and schools of herring inhabit the lagoon.
2. Only slightly further out from shore, the clumps of *Pocillopora* are so densely packed together that they lie virtually on top of one another. Competition for space at this site is obviously intense. Rottnest Island is the southernmost location that this species is known to grow. In fact it is quite remarkable that these animals are able to grow here so far south of their normal tropical or sub-tropical habitat.
3. Around the reef there are numerous wrasse species, such as moon wrasse, which appear to be painted in gorgeous colours. These species go through a variety of colour changes in their lifetime, as they change from juveniles to adults and females to males. As a result, it is often very difficult to tell which species you are looking at. You can also spot numerous red-lipped morwong, zebra fish, skipjack trevally, moonlighters, buffalo bream, scalyfin and horseshoe leatherjackets, to name just a few.
4. On your return to your boat or to the shore, see if you can spot one of the large and quite spectacular eagle rays that inhabit the area. They lounge around Parker Point in the hope of obtaining fish scraps from boats. The movement of their

graceful wings is reminiscent of a trapeze artist or dancer. As they cruise around, numerous fish can be seen fleeing from them, although they mostly feed on molluscs and crabs.

Caution areas: Avoid touching or otherwise damaging the delicate corals. Swell washing over the reef may result in cuts and abrasions.
Degree of difficulty: Easy.
Area's status: Marine conservation area within the Rottnest Island marine reserve. All marine life is protected.

Dave Burton, Carolyn Thomson and Peter Dans

WHAT IS A CORAL?

The basic component of a coral reef is the coral polyp. These animals take the form of a cylinder of tissue. Each is closed at the base and has a mouth at the other end that is surrounded by tentacles. The tentacles have stinging cells used to capture food such as plankton and also serve as a defence mechanism. Some species may exist as individual polyps, but most form colonies which live together as a single entity. Most corals feed at night and contract the polyps during the day, but some species may feed during the day. The three major coral groups are distinguished by the way in which they lay down their skeletons.

Hard corals produce a limestone skeleton by associating with tiny cells of algae known as zooanthellae. The microscopic zooanthellae find a safe haven in the living tissue of reef-building corals. Like other plants, they capture energy from the sun by photosynthesis, producing sugars and oils used by the coral host. They also help corals extract calcium carbonate from the surrounding water, which is used in reef-building. Corals with zooanthellae only flourish in warm clear low-nutrient water, so coral reefs are restricted to the tropics and sub-tropics.

Soft corals also have supporting structures of calcium carbonate but this takes a different form to hard corals. They contain small spicules within their tissue, rather than a continuous skeleton. They may also associate with zooanthellae.

Fan and whip corals, or **gorgonians**, have a hard skeletal core as well as calcium carbonate spicules. They rarely make use of symbiotic algae so, unlike their relatives, are not restricted to brightly-lit shallow waters. They often flourish in deep water, in caves and under overhangs where other corals are at a disadvantage.

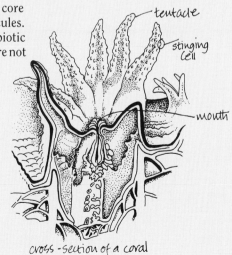

cross-section of a coral

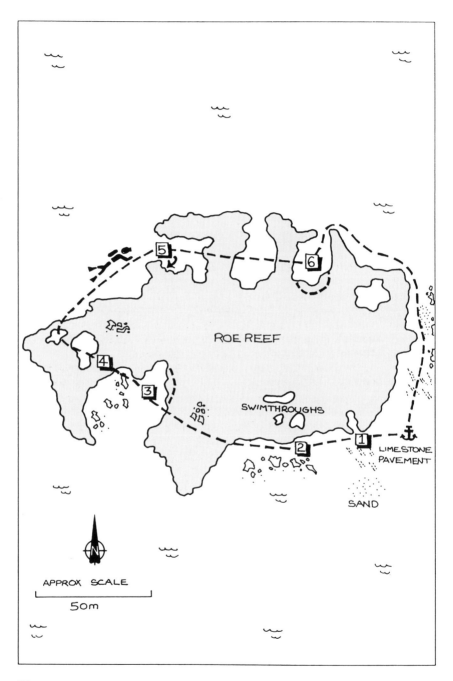

ROE REEF

SWIMTHROUGHS

LIMESTONE
PAVEMENT

SAND

N

APPROX SCALE

50m

Roe Reef

23

How to get there: By boat.
Depth: 15 metres.
Coordinates: Latitude 31°58'30" south, longitude 115°32'9" east.
Chart: DMH 412.

Roe Reef is as spectacular as any diving location near Perth. It has numerous underwater grottos and caverns. These are inhabited by marine life ranging from the large and impressive to the minute but colourful, such as tiny juvenile scalyfin.

1. Anchor in the sandy area south-east of Roe Reef. Swim towards the reef, where an opening leads in to a narrow canyon.
2. Continuing in a clockwise direction, you will find an area riddled with numerous swimthroughs, holes and ledges. Take some time to explore this area and its fish life. An impressive array of species can be seen, including white-barred boxfish, blue-lined leatherjackets, horseshoe leatherjackets, large schools of Woodward's pomfret, footballer sweep, western talma and old wives.
3. There is an interesting overhang to examine. Scalyfin protect their territories, schools of bronze bullseyes hover in caves, numerous western blue devils hide under ledges, harlequin fish, western foxfish, moon wrasse, red-lipped morwong, and smaller species such as black-headed pullers are present. The list is virtually endless and limited only by your knowledge of fish species. The best way to learn about the diversity of fish life and enhance enjoyment of your dive is to take a field guide on local fish on the boat and study it after you leave the water.
4. One of the highlights of this delightful reef is a large cave inhabited by large-snouted boarfish, zebra fish, mosaic leatherjackets and other colourful species.
5. The next point of interest is a swimthrough on the north-western part of the reef. You may see other animals of interest *en route*, including cuttlefish and brain coral colonies. You can see delicate but colourful nudibranchs nestled amongst the algae and other invertebrates, such as sea squirts and sponges.
6. Swim due east to find an overhang, then continue around the reef to return to your boat.

Caution areas: Swimming in to caves and under ledges can be hazardous. Take potential wind changes in to account when anchoring your vessel.
Degree of difficulty: Moderate.
Area's status: The waters around Rottnest Island are a marine reserve.

Dave Burton, Carolyn Thomson and Kevin Crane

Marmion Marine Park

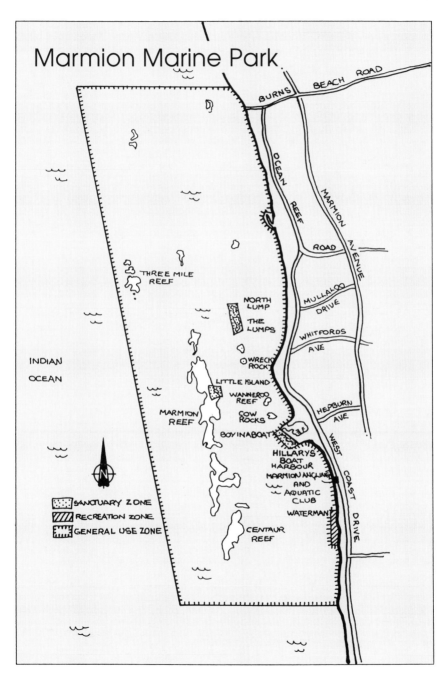

BEACH ROAD
BURNS
OCEAN REEF
MARMION AVENUE
ROAD
MULLALOO DRIVE
WHITFORDS AVE
HEPBURN AVE
WEST COAST DRIVE

THREE MILE REEF

NORTH LUMP
THE LUMPS
WRECK ROCK
LITTLE ISLAND
WANNEROO REEF
COW ROCKS
BOYINABOAT
MARMION REEF

HILLARYS BOAT HARBOUR
MARMION ANGLING AND AQUATIC CLUB
WATERMAN

CENTAUR REEF

INDIAN OCEAN

N

:::: SANCTUARY ZONE
/// RECREATION ZONE
GENERAL USE ZONE

99

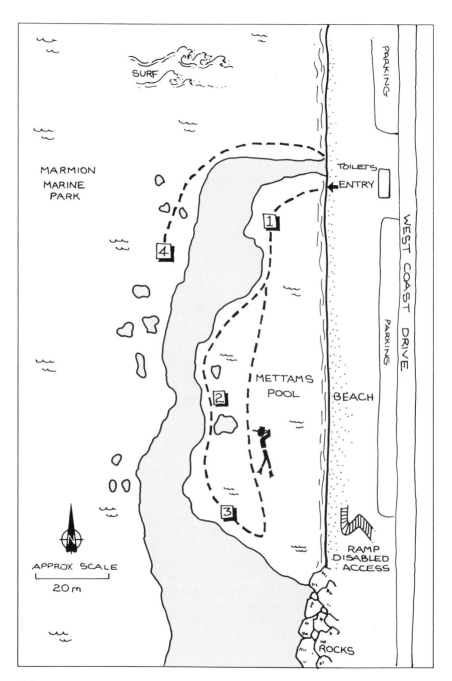

SURF

MARMION
MARINE
PARK

PARKING

TOILETS
ENTRY

1

4

2

METTAMS
POOL

BEACH

WEST COAST DRIVE

PARKING

3

N

APPROX SCALE
20 m

RAMP
DISABLED
ACCESS

ROCKS

Mettams Pool

24

How to get there: Park along West Coast Highway near the corner of Lynn Street in North Beach. Swim from the beach.
Depth: 1-2 metres inside the pool; 3-4 metres outside it.

This is a good family spot, ideal for the first time snorkeller or for introducing children to snorkelling. It is a protected pool within a barrier reef. There are also disabled access ramps to the beach. As well as the more noticeable attractions, such as fish, this dive is a good opportunity to pay attention to other life forms which are often overlooked.

1. The broken reef near the entry point is inhabited by a number of fish species. Of these, the red-lipped morwong are probably the largest and most noticeable.
2. Green, red and brown algae grow in the pool. Algae, or seaweeds, are very primitive life forms and are unrelated to seagrasses. Unlike seagrasses, they do not have roots, stems, leaves, flowers or fruit. Roots are unnecessary because the algae are anchored to rocks by holdfasts. They convert sunlight, chemical substances in sea water and carbon dioxide into proteins, fats and carbohydrates by means of photosynthesis and are an important food source for many fish and invertebrates. They reproduce by means of spores, which are released directly in to the water. Kelp and sargassum are two forms of brown algae that grow in the area. Sea lettuce is a bright-green, flat-leaved alga. Its bright green fronds are found on exposed rock platforms and shallow pools which are only covered at high tide. Aboriginal people used to prepare and eat this plant.
3. A reasonably good range of fish species reside within the pool, particularly in the holes and crevices in the southern section. They include red-lipped morwong, banded sweep, bullseyes, wrasse, schools of buffalo bream, juvenile herring, sea mullet and blowfish. You may also notice a few anemones growing within the pool. These animals are fixed to the reef at their base. Each has a mouth, surrounded by a ring of long, stinging tentacles used to catch and paralyse small sea creatures. Anemones are closely related to jellyfish.
4. There are fewer fish to see on the seaward side of the reef. Banded sweep are the most noticeable. There are a number of lumps riddled with caves and crevices in about three to four metres of water. If there is little swell, exploring this area is quite an enjoyable experience. However, the area would not be safe or comfortable for children.

Caution areas: *Surge can be strong on the outer edge of the reef. Beware of cobblers in the weed near the shore.*
Degree of difficulty: *Easy.*
Area's status: *Marmion Marine Park.*

Peter Dans and Carolyn Thomson

THE WRECK OF THE *CENTAUR*

On December 9, 1874 the *Centaur* was wrecked on a reef that now lies within the boundaries of the Marmion Marine Park. The sailing vessel struck the southernmost section of the Marmion Reef, about three kilometres offshore from North Beach, while en route to Fremantle.

The 30 metre long iron brig played an important role in the development of the infant colony, transporting galena (lead ore) from Champion Bay (Geraldton), which was then a thriving mining area, via Fremantle to Melbourne. It brought back vital supplies such as spirits, tobacco, nails, wagons, angora goats, and the colony's first quartz crushing battery in readiness for the anticipated gold boom.

The *Centaur* was carrying 200 tonnes of galena when it struck the reef at six and a half knots and became impaled on it. The nine crew and four passengers on board were able to scramble to safety, but five minutes after the lifeboats pulled away the ship crashed over and largely disappeared from view. At a subsequent inquiry the Captain, Frederick Brabham, was criticised for bringing the vessel too near the coast, and his license suspended for three months.

The *Centaur*'s remains still lie scattered around the submerged reef, the weed-covered starboard ribs sticking out from its base.

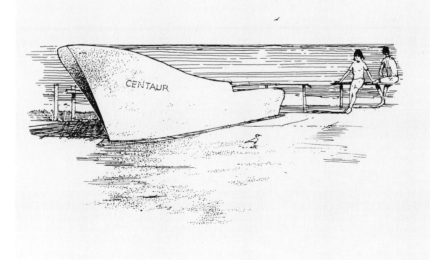

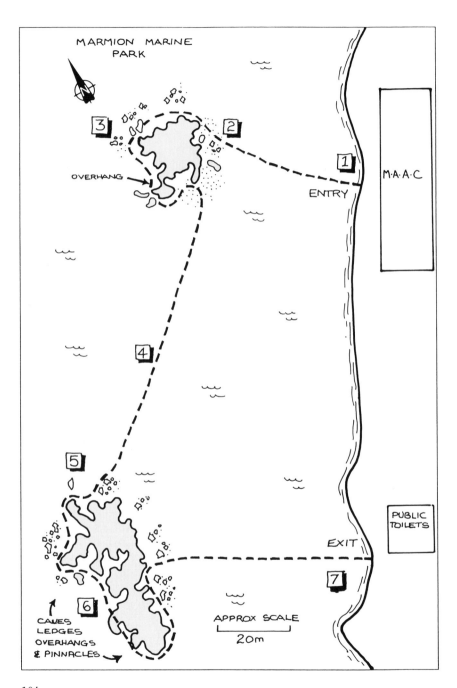

Offshore from Marmion Angling and Aquatic Club

25

How to get there: The Marmion Angling and Aquatic Club is on West Coast Highway a little south of Hillarys Boat Harbour. Limited parking is available near the club. Swim out to the reefs from shore.
Depth: 3-5 metres.

Marmion Angling and Aquatic Club is one of the most popular shore dives within the Marmion Marine Park. It is excellent for both SCUBA diving and snorkelling, although the combination of shallow depth and swell may make snorkelling more comfortable and less arduous. Be aware that the dive is very susceptible to swell and poor visibility.

1. Enter the water in front of the club and swim to the reef just offshore.
2. Circumnavigate the reef in an anti-clockwise direction. Sea lettuce and kelp are dominant on the eastern side of the reef and turbans and whelks can be seen. Pitted limestone lumps are encrusted with coralline algae, purple anemones and sea tulips (ascidians). The reef itself contains numerous small holes, inhabited by sponges and other invertebrate life.
3. The seaward side of the reef is about four metres deep. The deeper overhangs are inhabited by the usual fish species such as scalyfin, bullseyes, old wives, red-lipped morwong and banded sweep. Schools of herring cale, various wrasse, Port Jackson sharks and southern silverbellies may also be seen on this dive.
4. Swim to a second reef to the south. En route you will see rubble and holes containing shell graveyards, worn to sediment in many places, and algae in varying growth forms and colours. Sea squirts, sponges and sea urchins can be found amid the algae and rubble. Tiny anemones and small black, almost cylindrical, sea stars can be spotted on the areas of limestone pavement.
5. Take time to explore the reef, which has many shallow gullies and overhangs. There is a reasonably-sized swimthrough on the northern side.
6. The south-western section of this second, larger reef contains a maze of small caves, ledges, overhangs and pinnacles. It is by far the highlight of the dive.
7. Exit near the public toilets.

Caution areas: Many of the swimthroughs and caves could be dangerous in a swell greater than half a metre.
Degree of difficulty: Moderate.
Area's status: Lies within the Marmion Marine Park.

Peter Dans, Dave Burton and Kevin Crane

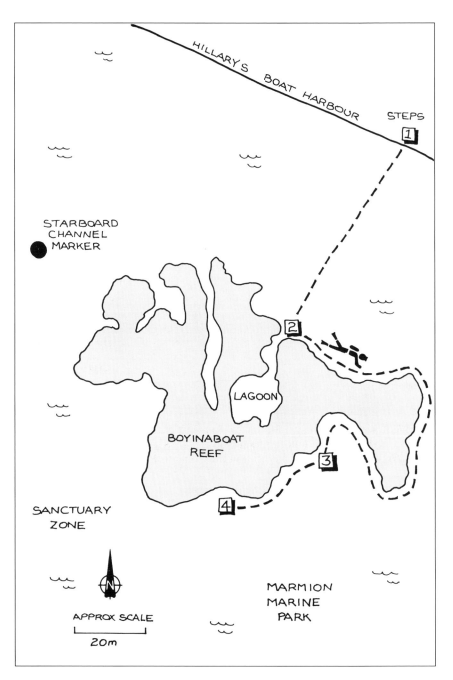

Boyinaboat Reef

26

How to get there: *Swim from the southern sea wall of Hillarys Boat Harbour.*
Depth: *4-6 metres.*

Boyinaboat Reef lies at the southern end of a chain of inshore reefs that formed the coastline thousands of years ago, when the sea level was lower. It was named because, when viewed from shore, its shape was once said to resemble a boy in a boat. With the construction of Hillarys Boat Harbour it is now just 75 metres from the sea wall and its accessibility and beauty has made it one of the most popular dive sites in Perth. It is also a good night dive. Although it is possible to snorkel the reef because it is relatively shallow, SCUBA diving is recommended to fully appreciate the variety of marine life.

Access to the reef is via the Hillarys southern breakwater. Park in the carpark near Underwater World, where it is best to prepare your equipment. Walk about 200 metres to the steps cut in to the wall. Ten underwater plaques have been placed at sites around the reef by the Department of Conservation and Land Management and provide information about marine ecosystems and marine life. The underwater nature trail takes about 60 minutes to complete.

1. Beginning at the rocky wall adjacent to the steps, swim about 75 metres to the reef. The reef itself is quite large and you may wish to sample a portion of it rather than trying to swim quickly around the whole reef.
2. Locate the first plaque near the point shown and swim in a clockwise direction around the reef. The southern side is richest in marine life. Kelp beds are common on the broken reef and reef lip, but the reef walls are almost totally covered by invertebrates such as sea squirts, anemones and sea fans. The diversity and colour is surprising.
3. Some very large encrusting sponges can be found, impressively covering whole rock faces. It is worth taking the time to examine the different colours and growth forms adopted by these animals. On Boyinaboat the colours range from pink, light blue, yellow, white, orange and many more. Living sponges look nothing like the bathroom sponge, which is only the skeleton of one particular group of sponges. These remarkable animals have no mouths or blood systems. Aristotle, some 2000 years ago, was the first to recognise the animal nature of sponges. In the sixteenth century, sponges were believed to be solidified sea foam and in the seventeenth century it was suggested that they were the homes of

marine worms. Otherwise, the general impression was that sponges belonged to the plant kingdom.

4. The trail ends with the "Wall Street" plaque. From here, you can either continue around the reef or swim back over it and through the lagoon. The many caverns and ledges on this reef simply teem with life. Polychaete worms, with their beautiful fans, are especially common. So are pencil urchins. The caverns also provide homes for many fish, the most common being scalyfin and red-lipped morwong. The scalyfin on this reef are particularly aggressive, probably because of the high number of divers that invade their homes. Other fish include western blue devils, old wives, banded sweep, crested morwong, horseshoe leatherjackets, dusky morwong, truncate coralfish, bullseyes, wrasse and red-striped cardinalfish. The reef top often comes alive with the frantic feeding of large schools of buffalo bream. Schools of footballer sweep create a colourful display. Blue and orange nudibranchs are common and add to the colour.

Caution areas: Swimming in to caverns and under ledges can be hazardous. Take care to avoid boat traffic and be sure to tow a dive flag.
Degree of difficulty: Moderate.
Area's status: Sanctuary zone within the Marmion Marine Park. Look at but don't touch marine animals and fish.

John Edwards, Kevin Crane, Carolyn Thomson and Rae Burrows

NUDIBRANCHS

Colourful nudibranchs (pronounced 'nudibranks') have fascinating life histories. Different species of these sea slugs have evolved diverse adaptations that enable them to survive in the marine environment. They are only distantly related to land slugs. Unlike other molluscs, they don't need to generate the huge amount of energy required to build and continually enlarge a shell.

All nudibranchs are carnivores. A group of nudibranchs known as aeolids feed mainly on sea anemones, hydroids, soft corals and hard reef corals, which have special stinging structures called nematocysts. As they feed, aeolid nudibranchs are able to remove undamaged nematocysts and store them in their bodies for future use. When attacked, they can discharge the stinging cells to deter their predators.

Many brightly-coloured species store distasteful and noxious chemicals in glands in their skin. One species eats a poisonous sponge and uses the toxins from its food as a defence against enemies. The bright colours probably serve as a warning to predators that they are poisonous.

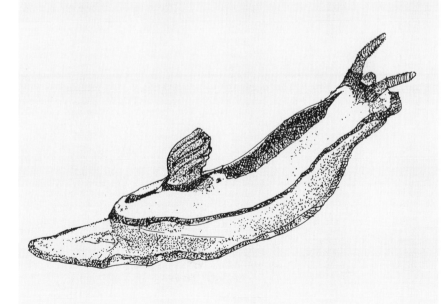

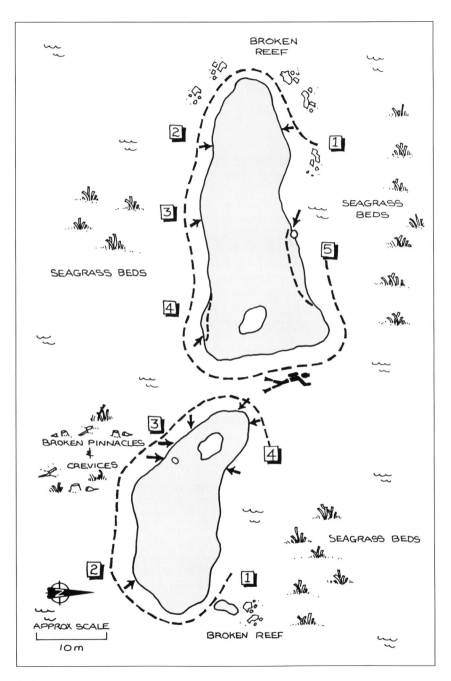

BROKEN
REEF

SEAGRASS
BEDS

SEAGRASS BEDS

BROKEN PINNACLES
&
CREVICES

SEAGRASS BEDS

APPROX SCALE

10 m

BROKEN REEF

Cow Rocks

How to get there: By boat from Hillarys Boat Harbour.
Depth: 6 metres.

Cow Rocks is probably the jewel of the chain of reefs lying one kilometre offshore. The invertebrate life here simply abounds. The site is only 500 metres west of Hillarys Boat Harbour. The rocks consist of two small reefs which are easily found, as each has a peak rising one metre above sea level. These can be seen as soon as you leave the harbour. Boats should be careful, however, not to anchor on the rich seagrass beds around this reef. To really appreciate the area, it is suggested you treat each lump as a separate dive and carry a dive torch with you.

The eastern lump (proceeding clockwise from the broken reef on the north-east):

1. Beautifully-coloured sea anemones can be seen on the broken reef. These animals use their stinging tentacles to capture food and for protection against predators.
2. On the reef itself, sponges, hydroids, gorgonian corals, polychaete worms, sea stars, feather stars, sea urchins, sea cucumbers and sea squirts are found in vast numbers. Feather stars usually have ten arms, each of which has many fine side branches that give them their feathery appearance. Although they look attractive to us, the arms mean death to the minute plants and animals they are used to trap. Unlike other echinoderms, feather stars have mouths facing upwards.
3. Fish life on this reef is also quite diverse. Scalyfin and red-lipped morwong are especially common, more so than on other reefs in the park. Red-lipped morwong seem to occupy nearly every available small crevice and show little interest in passing divers.
4. The reef itself is scarred with many small caves and crevices. They supply many micro-habitats and help explain the high diversity of this reef. Keep an eye open for comb jellies in the water. These exquisite creatures resemble jellyfish and are commonly encountered drifting in the currents around the limestone reefs of Western Australia. They are named for the comb-like rows of tiny hairs arranged along their bodies. Vibrations of these hairs produce waves of colour of descriptions. Like jellyfish, these animals have stinging cells, but they are greatly reduced and they are not dangerous.

The western lump has many interconnected caves, ledges and swimthroughs which demand further exploration. To explore this area, it is suggested that you proceed in an anti-clockwise direction from the broken reef on the north-west:

1. As you descend, you will notice the mass of sea anemones that seem to be littered around the broken reef. There are literally hundreds of them in many different colours.
2. At the bottom of the reef there are many tight ledges that reach several metres back. They provide a perfect hiding spot for the nocturnal cuttlefish.
3. The rich seagrass beds surrounding this reef also enhance the marine fauna on this reef.
4. As with other reefs, common fish species include old wives, bronze bullseyes, banded sweep and buffalo bream.
5. There are also a number of large brain coral colonies.

Caution areas: *Do not dive when there is a moderate swell with wind greater than 15 knots.*
Degree of difficulty: *Moderate.*
Area's status: *Lies within the Marmion Marine Park.*

Kevin Crane

WRASSE AND "CLEANER FISH"

Wrasse are amongst the most striking and colourful reef fish. They range from small to very large and there are at least 400 species. All are carnivorous. Many species are capable of radical colour changes with growth and sex reversal.

Some small species of wrasse act as "cleaner fish", which remove parasites from the heads and gills of larger carnivorous fish such as groper, snapper, parrotfish and eels. The valuable services provided by the smaller fish save them from being eaten. Because the cleaner fish are small they tend to stay in one place, which becomes recognised as a cleaner station. The larger fish make regular visits to these stations to be cleaned. Cleaning stations are very important to the health and welfare of whole communities of fish.

The blue-streaked wrasse is one such cleaner fish and it performs an elaborate dance to advertise its services. The dance attracts fish which allow the wrasse to enter their mouths and gills for cleaning. This species can be seen in the northern half of Australia, but several small colonies have been observed on reefs at Rottnest Island. The king wrasse is the most common cleaner fish in southern waters.

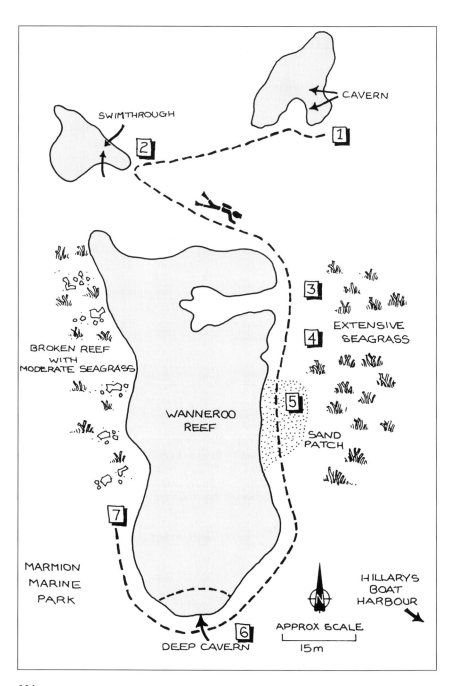

CAVERN

SWIMTHROUGH

1

2

3

EXTENSIVE
SEAGRASS

4

BROKEN REEF
WITH
MODERATE SEAGRASS

5

SAND
PATCH

WANNEROO
REEF

7

MARMION
MARINE
PARK

HILLARYS
BOAT
HARBOUR

N

6

DEEP CAVERN

APPROX SCALE
15m

Wanneroo Reef

28

How to get there: By boat from Hillarys Boat Harbour.
Depth: 6 metres.

Wanneroo Reef is north-west of Hillarys at 31°49' south, 115°43'30" east. The main reef is about 90 metres long, with two lumps at the northern end. The maximum depth around the reef is six metres, with the reef flat being exposed.

1. If there are onshore winds, start on the eastern side, beginning at the north-eastern lump. Marine life here is similar to the main reef, with a variety of anemones and gorgonian corals.
2. Another more westerly lump is worth a look, or go straight to the main reef.
3. The best diving is on the eastern side of the reef, especially at the north-eastern end, where some spectacular caverns can be found. The reef itself provides the most diverse array of marine life. The reef lip is dominated by kelp. On the reef walls, however, invertebrate life proliferates. A variety of colourful sponges, gorgonians, hard corals, feather stars and sea squirts can be found. Fern-like bryozoans feed by filtering minute plants and animals from the water, but may themselves fall prey to predators such as nudibranchs. Close inspection of these animals is rewarding. Cowries are quite common, especially on the north-eastern section. You should not remove these animals from the marine park. Leave them here where they belong for others to enjoy.
4. Seagrass beds predominate on the sandy areas around the reef, and a variety of marine life can be found here. Sea stars, sea cucumbers and many fish species are plentiful. These rich seagrass beds enhance the animal life on this reef.
5. Look for a large sand patch, which you can use to orientate yourself. Fish life on this reef is diverse. Schooling rough bullseyes provide quite a spectacle. Scalyfin are common. These territorial fish diligently defend their watery homes. Old wives, crested morwong and red-lipped morwong can also be seen.
6. On the southern end of the reef is a deep cavern.
7. On the seaward side there is broken reef, where turf algae is predominant. Invertebrates include a variety of quite beautiful anemones, sea urchins, sea stars and sea cucumbers. The jumping blenny and schooling buffalo bream are common fish.

Caution areas: Swimming in to caverns and under ledges can be hazardous.
Degree of difficulty: Moderate.
Area's status: Lies within the Marmion Marine Park.

Kevin Crane and Dave Burton

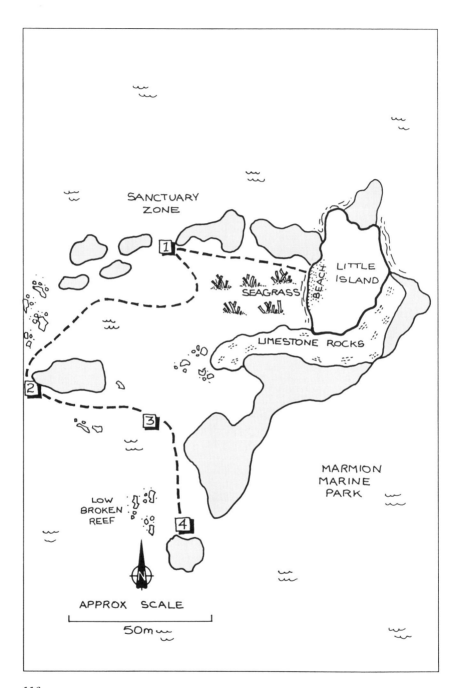

SANCTUARY ZONE

1

SEAGRASS

BEACH

LITTLE ISLAND

LIMESTONE ROCKS

2

3

MARMION MARINE PARK

LOW BROKEN REEF

4

APPROX SCALE

50m

N

Little Island

29

How to get there: By boat from Hillarys Boat Harbour.
Depth: 5 metres.

Little Island is two kilometres north-west of Hillarys Boat Harbour. It is a favourite resting place for Australian sea lions. The limestone reef, and hence the best diving, is on the western side of the island, with a maximum depth of six metres. Little Island also has an underwater nature trail, established by the Department of Conservation and Land Management. The trail has 10 plaques that describe various aspects of marine ecology, and is suitable for both SCUBA diving and snorkelling.

The best anchorage is in the large sandy area of sea floor on the eastern (mainland) side of the island. It is then only a short swim to the dive site. Only brief landings of about 10 minutes are allowed on the island, to allow the sea lions free passage to and from the beach.

1. Swim about 30 metres west from the sandy beach of the island, along the intertidal reef, where there are some interesting swimthroughs and caves. There are two plaques to find in this area - one on seals and sea lions and the second on seagrass. While exploring this area, divers may encounter sea lions. As the island is not a breeding area, there is usually no need for concern, but caution is advised. Divers can simply sit back and watch these gracious animals at play. However, they are wild animals and capable of delivering a nasty bite if aggravated. It is advised therefore that, when sea lions are in the water, divers keep their arms close to their bodies and don't attempt to touch them. If a sea lion attempts to nudge you, he is probably letting you know that you're invading his territory, so if this occurs it is time to leave the water.

2. Swim west until you reach the edge of the reef, locating three plaques on the way. The limestone reefs to the west of Little Island are lined with marine life. On the sandy areas, seagrass beds are abundant, providing a nursery for many young fish. The fragmented reef houses a variety of marine life. Kelp beds are dominant, but there is also a large amount of sea lettuce. The surface of the reef is almost totally covered by either turf or coralline algae, with few bare patches. Red algae is especially common underneath the cover of the kelp beds.

3. Travelling in an easterly direction towards the intertidal reef to the south of Little Island, you should be able to locate two more plaques. Invertebrate life throughout the dive site is diverse. Sponges, gorgonians, hydroids, sea urchins and sea

squirts can all be found in large numbers underneath ledges and in caves.
4. Head south until you reach the most southerly lump shown on the map. The last three plaques can be located in this area. Fish life is diverse around Little Island, although smaller reef fish predominate. More than 136 species of fish are found in the Marmion Marine Park. The seagrass meadows that grow in sandy areas around the island also support a huge range of animals such as bailer shells. Their egg cases are occasionally found attached to rocks or other shells. These large, translucent sponge-like cases contain more than 100 developing shells.

Caution areas: *Swimming in to caves and under ledges can be hazardous.*
Degree of difficulty: *Easy to moderate, depending on conditions.*
Area's status: *Sanctuary zone in the Marmion Marine Park. Look but don't touch. All marine life in sanctuary zones is protected.*

Kevin Crane and John Edwards

RAYS

Rays are among the most graceful animals that inhabit our underwater world. Most have venomous spines attached to their tails. The venom of some species, such as the smooth stingray and black stingray, is particularly potent, and can affect the circulatory system and cause heart failure. Despite their fearsome reputation, rays are usually not aggressive, but care should be taken not to tread on them by accident. Electric rays, such as the numbfish, have organs along their backs that can deliver a powerful electric shock if they are handled or trodden on.

Like sharks, to which they are closely related, rays do not have true bones but cartilage and have an ancient lineage that can be traced back 350 million years. As with many shark species, almost all types of rays hatch their eggs within the uterus and then give birth to live young. They emerge tail-first and their venom spines are rubbery at birth, presumably to prevent the mother being impaled.

The manta rays found in tropical waters are large and powerful and also have a reputation for being dangerous, but they are in fact plankton feeders. They use a pair of slender feeding flaps on each side of the head to direct food towards their mouths as they cruise through swarms of plankton.

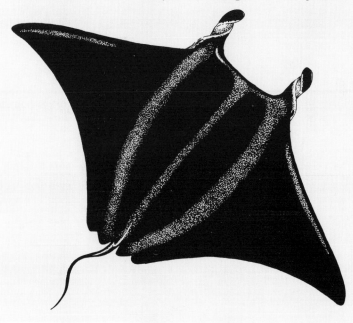

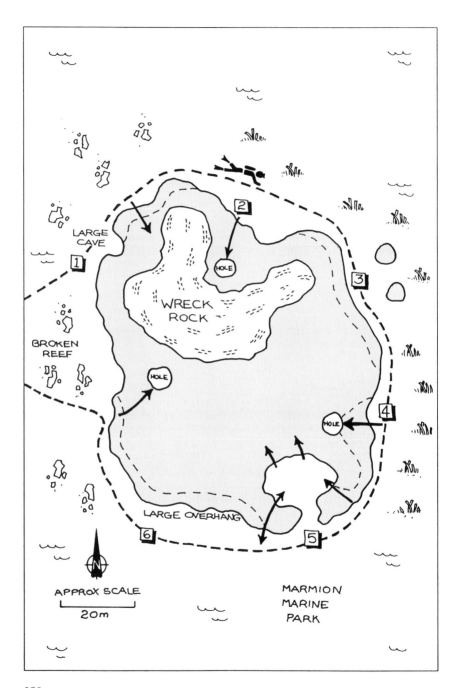

LARGE CAVE

1

2

HOLE

3

WRECK ROCK

BROKEN REEF

HOLE

HOLE

4

LARGE OVERHANG

6

5

N

APPROX SCALE

20m

MARMION MARINE PARK

Wreck Rock

30

How to get there*: By boat from Hillarys Boat Harbour.*
Depth*: 8 metres.*
Coordinates*: Latitude 31°48'15" south, longitude 115°43'5" east .*

Wreck Rock features numerous crevices and overhangs lined with a diverse range of invertebrates. This is an excellent dive that is close to Hillarys.

1. Beginning on the western side of Wreck Rock, just beyond an area of broken reef, you will come across a large cave, followed by a ledge and more broken reef. Bailer shells may be seen in areas of seagrass or broken reef, feeding on starfish and other molluscs. They have an intricately-patterned slug-like foot.
2. Continue around the reef in a clockwise direction and locate a swimthrough, leading to a hole.
3. Opposite some large lumps there is a fairly long ledge. Other marine life seen here includes sea cucumbers, sponges, hydroids, gorgonians, hard corals, anemones, polychaete worms, starfish, feather stars, sea urchins and nudibranchs.
4. Further along the reef there is a swimthrough cavern leading to a hole. Boldly patterned cowries hide in nooks and crannies in and around the reef. These shellfish have highly polished and unusually thick shells that are generally encased in a fleshy camouflaging mantle. Cowries living within the marine park are protected species and may not be removed.
5. On the south-eastern part of the reef you will see a large swimthrough surrounded by ledges. Fish species recorded here include rough bullseyes, old wives, whiting, banded sweep, buffalo bream, red-lipped morwong, common scalyfin, black-headed pullers, brown-spotted wrasse and Shaw's boxfish.
6. You will come across a large ledge. A species of flatworm related to the Spanish dancer has been seen on this reef. Only a few centimetres long, it too resembles the fluttering skirt of a flamenco dancer. The leaf-like black body is skirted with a strip of brilliant orange. These delicate animals hide in mud, under stones, in empty shells and among seaweed, sponges and corals. They are carnivorous and swim by undulating their body margins.

Caution areas*: Swimming in to caves and under ledges can be hazardous.*
Degree of difficulty*: Moderate.*
Area's status*: Lies within the Marmion Marine Park.*

Dirk Erler, John Edwards, Carolyn Thomson, Peter Dans and Kevin Crane

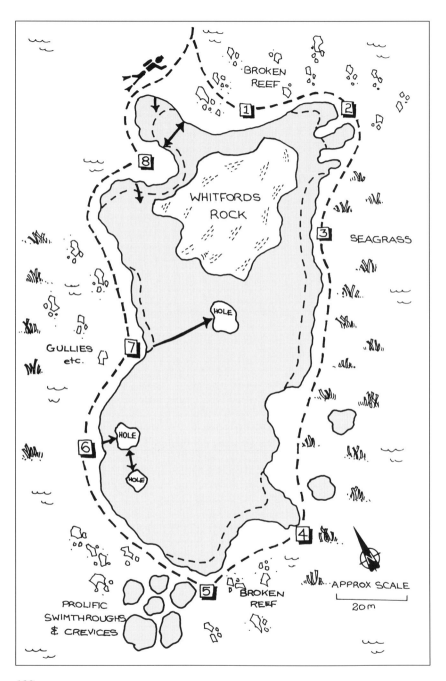

Whitfords Rock

31

How to get there: By boat from Hillarys Boat Harbour.
Depth: 7 metres.
Coordinates: Latitude 31°48'2" south, longitude 115°43'1" east.

Whitfords Rock, just north of Wreck Rock, is easy to find, close to Hillarys Boat Harbour and offers a rewarding dive. There are many intricate overhangs, ledges and swimthroughs. The south-western side, in particular, has some spectacular limestone formations.

1. Lying at the northern end of Whitfords Rock is an area of broken reef inhabited by common scalyfin, red-lipped morwong, various wrasse species, banded sweep, bullseyes, buffalo bream and whiting.
2. Continuing around the reef in a clockwise direction, you will encounter crevices and caves which are lined with almost all forms of invertebrates. Gorgonians, ascidians, sponges and anemones are prolific.
3. A very long ledge lies along the reef's eastern side. A closer look at some of the marine life may reveal brightly-coloured nudibranchs. These sea slugs belong to the same group as shells, squid and octopuses. They are hermaphrodites and can mate with any other individual. To the left there are beds of seagrass. Sea urchins are present in the sand and rubble surrounding the reef.
4. Find another ledge crammed with invertebrate life. This section of the reef has numerous delicate gorgonians, or sea fans. These animals use their tentacles to intercept food. They are all positioned at right angles to the current, to maximise the capture of plankton and other microscopic food particles.
5. A series of smaller lumps to the south of the reef contain prolific swimthroughs and crevices.
6 & 7. Explore several swimthroughs and caves that go through to holes in the middle of the reef. Marine life includes black-spotted catsharks and stingrays. Catsharks are small (usually less than three feet long), harmless to people and beautifully patterned. Most species have exotic stripes, bars and mottling.
8. More ledges and swimthroughs can be found on the north-western end of the reef.

Caution areas: Swimming in to caves and under ledges can be hazardous.
Degree of difficulty: Moderate.
Area's status: Lies within the Marmion Marine Park.

Dirk Erler, John Edwards and Carolyn Thomson

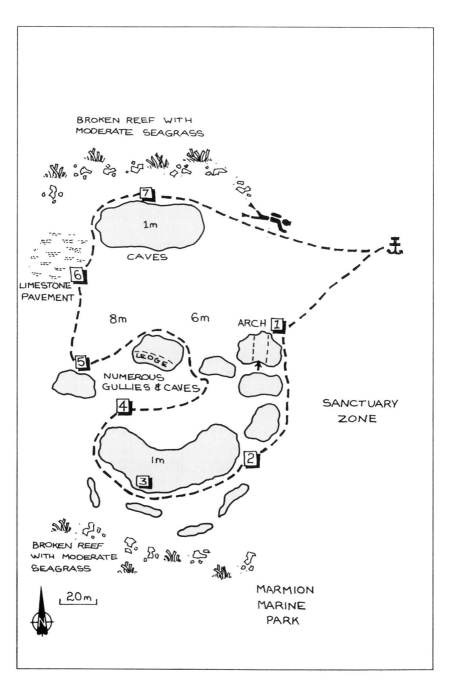

BROKEN REEF WITH
MODERATE SEAGRASS

7

1m

CAVES

6

LIMESTONE
PAVEMENT

8m   6m   ARCH 1

5

LEDGE

NUMEROUS
GULLIES & CAVES

4

SANCTUARY
ZONE

1m

2

3

BROKEN REEF
WITH MODERATE
SEAGRASS

20m

N

MARMION
MARINE
PARK

North Lump

How to get there: By boat from Hillarys Boat Harbour.
Depth: 8 metres.

North Lump is four and a half kilometres north of Hillarys Boat Harbour at 31°47'18" south, 115°42'48" east. This entirely submerged reef offers a rewarding dive within a small area, with interesting arches, caves and tunnels and excellent invertebrate life. It is suggested that you anchor on the leeward side. The reef is not a complete block but composed of many rocky outcrops interspersed with numerous gullies and canyons.

1. Due to the lack of habitat, there are no seagrasses in the immediate vicinity of the reef. Kelp beds instead occupy most of the rocky habitat. A variety of coralline and red algae can be found beneath the kelp. Swimming in a south-westerly direction from the suggested anchorage, you will come across a small arch and cave.
2 & 3. Continuing south past some small lumps, locate a larger reef. On top of this reef, in about a metre of water, there is a large indentation that has become overgrown with hard, blue encrusting coral. It is quite impressive and well worth searching for.
4. To the north of this larger lump, explore an area riddled with numerous gullies and caves. Invertebrate life on the reef is rich, especially on reef walls and under ledges. A diverse array of sponges, hydroids, gorgonians, feather stars and sea squirts can be found. Because of the limited space, there is 100 per cent cover of marine life. Other invertebrates include anemones, polychaete worms, sea stars, nudibranchs and octopuses. Lying north of these interesting gullies is another small lump that drops away to six or seven metres. Beneath it is a ledge that may harbour a Port Jackson shark. These harmless but spectacular fish have attractive markings and a bony ridge above their eyes.
5. Schooling fish, such as rough bullseyes, buffalo bream, tailor, yellow-finned whiting and tuna, are common throughout North Lump. Reef fish include western blue devils, scalyfin, western morwong, sand bass and old wives. Stingrays are fairly common in the marine park. These graceful fish use their pectoral wings to dig in to the sand in search of food such as crustaceans and other bottom-dwelling creatures. These are quickly sucked in to the mouth and ground to pieces. Stingrays have venomous spines that they use for protection but they are not dangerous unless molested.

6. En route to the most northerly lump is an area of limestone pavement. A closer look may reveal marine animals such as sea urchins and shellfish sheltering in this area.
7. Circumnavigate the large limestone reef submerged about a metre below the surface before returning to your boat. You will see a similar suite of marine life to that seen elsewhere on the dive.

Caution areas: Do not dive this reef if the wind is greater than 10 knots or if there is a moderate swell.
Degree of difficulty: Moderate.
Area's status: Sanctuary zone within the Marmion Marine Park. Look but don't touch. All marine life in sanctuary zones is protected.

Kevin Crane and John Edwards

UMBRELLA OF SAFETY

Two fish species that associate with jellyfish when young are the mosaic leatherjacket and trevally. The jellyfish provide shelter, transportation and food, in the form of plankton killed and trapped by their stinging tissue. The young fish are immune to the stinging tentacles and can even eat them, despite the stings being toxic to other animals. The association does not appear to benefit the jellyfish, nor does it seem to do them any great harm.

Net-patterned jellyfish, with their tiny hangers-on and ballerina-like movements, begin to appear in Perth waters during late March and early April. Trevally cluster up front near the bell, with leatherjackets bringing up the rear. Immature leatherjackets also associate with spotted jellyfish, mosaic jellyfish, saucer jellyfish and hairy stingers. They leave their hosts when they are a few centimetres long to settle around jetty piles and other structures, then move to deeper waters as they mature. So next time you see a jellyfish in the ocean, see if you can spot any tiny hitchhikers.

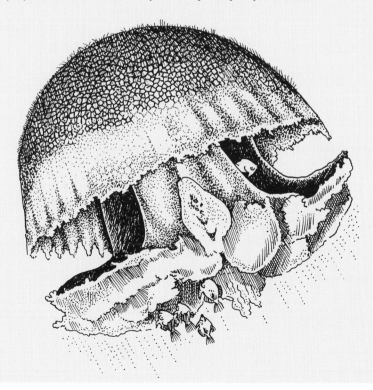

GASCOYNE

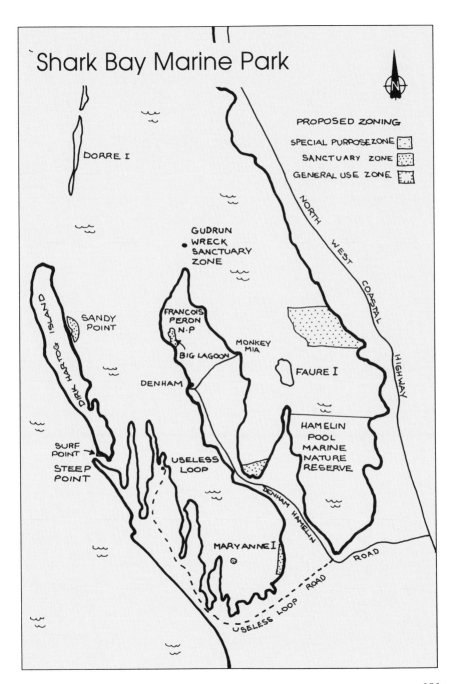

Shark Bay Marine Park

PROPOSED ZONING

SPECIAL PURPOSE ZONE
SANCTUARY ZONE
GENERAL USE ZONE

DORRE I

GUDRUN WRECK SANCTUARY ZONE

SANDY POINT

FRANCOIS PERON N·P

MONKEY MIA

BIG LAGOON

FAURE I

DENHAM

DIRK HARTOG ISLAND

NORTH WEST COASTAL HIGHWAY

SURF POINT

STEEP POINT

USELESS LOOP

HAMELIN POOL MARINE NATURE RESERVE

DENHAM HAMELIN

MARYANNE I

ROAD

USELESS LOOP ROAD

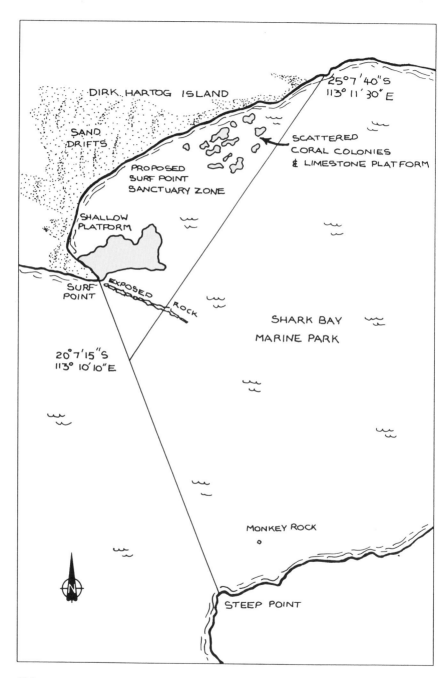

DIRK HARTOG ISLAND

25°7'40"S
113°11'30"E

SAND
DRIFTS

SCATTERED
CORAL COLONIES
& LIMESTONE PLATFORM

PROPOSED
SURF POINT
SANCTUARY ZONE

SHALLOW
PLATFORM

SURF
POINT

EXPOSED
ROCK

SHARK BAY
MARINE PARK

20°7'15"S
113°10'10"E

MONKEY ROCK
o

N

STEEP POINT

Surf Point

33

How to get there: By boat from Denham. Charters available.
Depth: 3-4 metres

Coral patches at Surf Point, south of Dirk Hartog Island, are likely to be set aside as a sanctuary area within the Shark Bay Marine Park. The area will be used as a benchmark for scientists to monitor any changes to other areas in the Bay. It is therefore a good place to see an undisturbed community of marine plants and animals. It is known particularly for its beautiful egg and tiger cowries, but snorkellers should remember to admire them and leave them there for others to enjoy.

It is suggested that divers concentrate on exploring the coral communities in the eastern part of the sanctuary zone. The area is in relatively shallow water which is protected from oceanic swells by a rocky platform reef. A good assemblage of both hard and soft corals can be found. There are communities of vase corals, plate corals and a great variety of staghorn species. This site has the most diverse coral communities in the marine park, probably due to more favourable conditions for coral growth at South Passage.

A wide range of tropical fish species can be seen at Surf Point, including a variety of parrotfish, butterflyfish, wrasse, angelfish and snapper. Baldchin groper are fairly common. As the name suggests, baldchin groper can be distinguished by their very pale chins. These large fish reach 90 centimetres long and can weigh up to seven kilograms. Blennies and gobies can also be seen. Gobies are common in sandy areas along the fringes of the reef where they may inhabit burrows. At least 323 species of fish inhabit South Passage, which is particularly diverse when compared to other major coral reef communities such as the Abrolhos Islands area. There are also high densities of invertebrates, including sea cucumbers.

Caution areas: Dive only on a slack tide. Take care not to anchor on the fragile corals.
Degree of difficulty: Moderate.
Area's status: Proposed sanctuary zone within the Shark Bay Marine Park.
Look at but do not touch marine life.

Carolyn Thomson

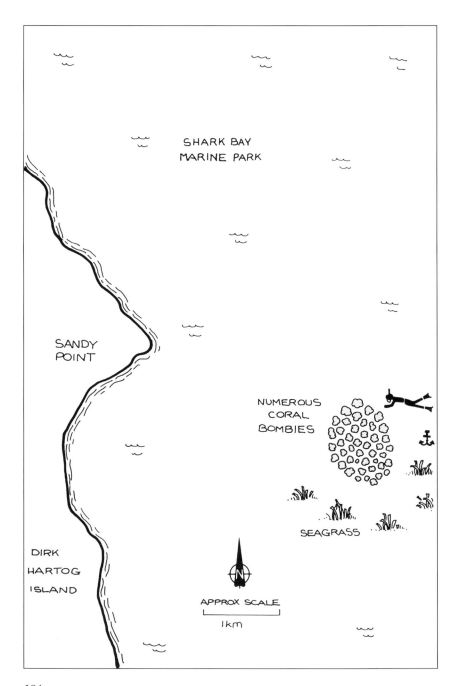

SHARK BAY
MARINE PARK

SANDY
POINT

NUMEROUS
CORAL
BOMBIES

SEAGRASS

DIRK
HARTOG
ISLAND

APPROX SCALE
1km

Sandy Point

34

How to get there*: By boat from Denham. Charters available.*
Depth*: 3-4 metres.*

The coral and fish communities of Sandy Point are in a proposed sanctuary zone. This excellent snorkelling area is very sheltered. It lies on the eastern side of Dirk Hartog Island at 25°43'24" south and 113°04'36" east. Numerous species of blue, purple, green and brown staghorn corals grow in a great diversity of forms. In one area there is a virtual garden of beautiful blue staghorn coral. Brain corals and plate corals can also be seen. You may see brain corals with polyps extended and feeding during the day. There is such a diversity of corals, in a kaleidoscope of colours and forms, that this is a good place to see how many different varieties and growth forms you can distinguish.

Fish species in the area include estuary cod, many species of brightly-coloured wrasse such as cleaner fish and green moon wrasse, scissortail sergeant, lined butterfly fish, varieties of surgeonfish and brightly-coloured angelfish.

Green and loggerhead turtles also inhabit the area. In Australian waters, herbivorous green turtles are more numerous than other marine turtles, which are carnivores. However, in some other parts of the world, such as the United States, they are classed as endangered. Individual turtles are common in Shark Bay all year round and congregations of turtles can be seen from the end of July, although the start of the breeding season is usually later. At mating time, males usually cluster around and compete for females, which inevitably breed with more than one male. Within a short time, the female lays her first eggs on the beach, repeating this on a fortnightly basis up to six or even eight times.

Surrounding the coral communities are seagrasses - which are the force driving the marine ecosystem of Shark Bay. They stabilise Shark Bay's largely sandy bottom, while seaweeds and some animals use the seagrass as a handy attachment point. Well over 100 species of plants and animals grow directly on the Shark Bay seagrasses. A good many more use the shelter it provides to protect them against predators. Seagrasses are more closely related to land plants than they are to seaweeds. They have adapted entirely to submerged living and even produce underwater flowers. The flowers are barely noticeable and may only last for a short time. Pollination occurs underwater and the currents convey the pollen from flower to flower.

The meadows are a nursery area for numerous species of fish and crustaceans. Dugongs feed on seagrasses directly, including species such as wire weed (*Amphibolis*

135

antarctica). These rotund mammals use their snouts to root in to the sea bottom and extract seagrass rhizomes. You may see the irregular wandering tracks they leave on seagrass beds. You may even see a dugong. Their hearing is excellent, allowing them to detect boats and other disturbances at a distance, and they may respond to the presence of a boat or swimmer by coming to investigate. In fact, the shallow marine environment of Shark Bay has one of the largest and most secure populations of dugongs in the world, with an estimated 10,000 animals. Traditionally, turtles and dugongs formed an important part of the diet of Aboriginal people but in Shark Bay these animals are not subject to as much hunting pressure as in other parts of the world.

On the way to the dive site, you may see humpback whales from July to October. Humpback whales are recovering from whaling, and sightings are bound to become more frequent as they increase in abundance. If you cut the engines of your boat and they are in a playful mood, they may be encouraged to approach of their own accord.

Caution areas: *Only dive this site on a slack tide.*
Degree of difficulty: *Easy to moderate, depending on conditions.*
Area's status: *Proposed sanctuary zone within the Shark Bay Marine Park.*
Look at but do not touch marine life.

Carolyn Thomson, Mike O'Day and Bill Cuthbert,
with assistance from the WA Fisheries Department

THE WRECK OF THE *GUDRUN*

The *Gudrun*, the biggest wooden shipwreck found off Western Australia, sank in 1901, carrying a load of jarrah from Bunbury to England. The ship was deliberately scuttled with more than a metre of water in its hold, after it had been sabotaged by the ship's carpenter. He admitted drilling a four centimetre hole though its bottom. The wreck was only rediscovered in 1989, when Paul Anderson, a Canadian studying dugongs in Shark Bay, found her on the sand flats north of Cape Peron in the Francois Peron National Park.

Today the wreck lies in about six metres of water, 5.3 nautical miles north of Cape Peron. It is within the Shark Bay Marine Park, and a special sanctuary zone extends 500 metres around the wreck to protect the site. Artefacts can't be removed and line fishing and spearfishing are not permitted. However, the tides can be very dangerous. Novice divers should only dive this site with a charter operator.

The *Gudrun* is one of Western Australia's largest untouched wrecks in shallow waters. The hull is buried largely intact up to a metre in the soft sands, but anchors, fastenings, deck knees and so on are visible. The remains, however, do not project much more than a metre above the sea bed and can be compared to an eggshell that has been opened up and flattened.

The wreck is 65 by 20 metres, with another 20 by eight metre section nearby. Because of its relatively untouched wreckage, stunning marine life, remote and romantic location and history, Maritime Museum archaeologists rate it as one of the State's best wreck dives. It has become home to a rich variety of fish and marine life, including marine turtles, giant groper, stingrays, spotted cod, many species of trevally and sweetlips.

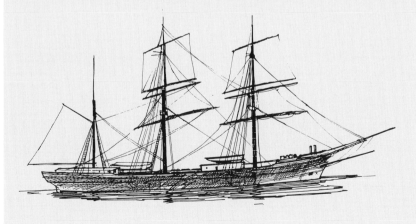

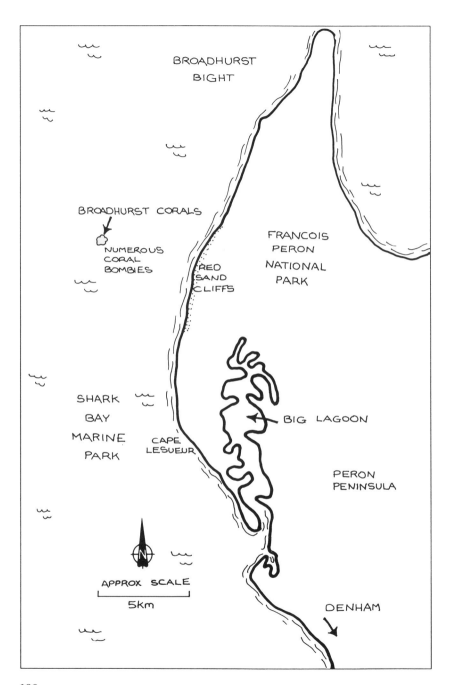

BROADHURST
BIGHT

BROADHURST CORALS

NUMEROUS
CORAL
BOMBIES

RED
SAND
CLIFFS

FRANCOIS
PERON

NATIONAL
PARK

SHARK
BAY

MARINE
PARK

CAPE
LESUEUR

BIG LAGOON

PERON
PENINSULA

N

APPROX SCALE
5km

DENHAM

Broadhurst Corals

35

How to get there: By boat from Denham or any of the boat launching sites in Francois Peron National Park. Charters available.
Depth: 3-4 metres.

The Broadhurst corals can be likened to a sandy football oval covered with growths of corals. Each of these communities contains numerous individuals, which are all genetically identical. They were formed by asexual reproduction from a single ancestor. The Broadhurst patch is around 500 metres in diameter, and swarms with colourful sea life. Many species of staghorn, brain and plate corals vie for attention. There are also numerous soft corals. A bright purple sponge growing throughout the area is notable. As the depth is only three to four metres there is no need to dive on SCUBA. The site can be located at 25°38'13" south and 113°22'14" east.

Rather than anchoring on the patch, which would risk damaging the reef, a drift over the patch with a shallow draught boat (with a driver on board) is recommended.

Fish species in the area include many species of brightly-coloured wrasse such as cleaner fish and green moon wrasse, scissortail sergeant, lined butterflyfish and varieties of surgeonfish. Surgeonfish are named because of the scalpel-like spine on each side of their tail base, which can be used in defense. There are also many brightly-coloured angelfish sheltering within the numerous coral communities. Some species of angelfish can make a loud drumming sound that can be heard by divers. These tropical fish are usually territorial and live in and around coral reefs.

Green turtles and dugongs also inhabit the area and you may be rewarded with an encounter. Shark Bay's famous dolphins often frolick here. These mammals are highly social and live in small groups. Members of a group change from time to time and they assist each other in activities such as fish herding and calf rearing.

Caution areas: Only dive this site on a slack tide.
Degree of difficulty: Easy to moderate, depending on conditions.
Area's status: Lies within the Shark Bay Marine Park.

Carolyn Thomson, Mike O'Day and Bill Cuthbert,
with assistance from the WA Fisheries Department

Ningaloo Marine Park

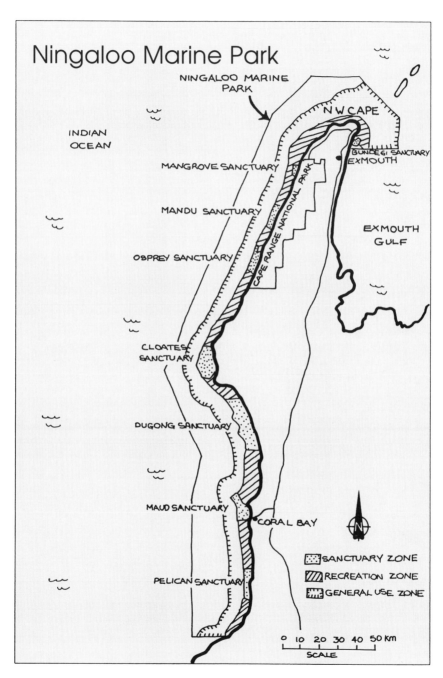

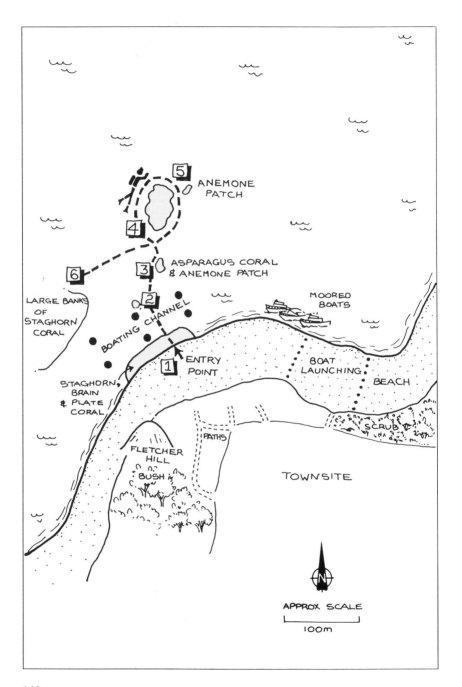

ANEMONE PATCH

ASPARAGUS CORAL & ANEMONE PATCH

LARGE BANKS OF STAGHORN CORAL

BOATING CHANNEL

MOORED BOATS

ENTRY POINT

BOAT LAUNCHING

BEACH

STAGHORN, BRAIN & PLATE CORAL

SCRUB

FLETCHER HILL

BUSH

PATHS

TOWNSITE

N

APPROX SCALE

100m

Coral Bay foreshore

36

How to get there: *Coral Bay is 154 kilometres south of Exmouth. The dive site begins directly from the settlement foreshore.*
Depth: *Up to 6 metres at high tide.*

Coral Bay is an excellent site for novice snorkellers and photographers, but experienced divers will no doubt enjoy it as well, as there is so much to see and minimal effort is required. A large variety of coral and fish life can be seen, with the coral beginning only metres from the foreshore.

The area from the five knot sign (Fletcher Hill) around to the area in front of the Coral Bay Hotel provides safe and comfortable snorkelling in depths of one to three metres. Despite the site being relatively shallow, many people prefer to explore it on SCUBA, which allows them to closely examine all the nooks and crannies. Large cabbage corals, staghorn, asparagus and brain corals abound. Blue-spotted fantail stingrays (colourful rays decorated with bright blue spots) and sailfin catfish can be easily seen in sandy areas.

1. Enter the water in the area densely packed with staghorn, brain and plate corals, just off the beach a little north of Fletcher Hill.
2. Just beyond this area there is a boating channel, clearly marked by buoys. You need to surface and swim across the channel, towing a dive flag and taking great care that there are no boats. Swim to the large dead coral bombie near one of the buoys. Although the original bombie is now dead, it is being recolonised by small staghorn corals and other marine organisms.
3. Nearby there is a patch of asparagus coral and anemones that is well worth inspecting.
4. Further out, a large garden of lavender coral teems with fish life. This is a kind of *Pocillopora* coral, which is commonly found in shallow water habitats north of Rottnest Island. The fish life ranges from large schools of spangled emperor and drummers, damselfish, moon wrasse, parrotfish and many other members of the wrasse family. The coral provides homes for predatory moray eels and lionfish. The latter are strikingly attractive but they have venomous spines that can cause painful wounds, so be sure to look but not touch.
5. Examine another anemone patch just north of the lavender coral. Look for the resident anemonefish. These attractive fish actually bathe in the tentacles of the anemones without fear of being stung, thereby gaining protection from larger predators with no such immunity.

6. If the tide is high you will be able to make your way over to the large banks of blue staghorn coral. During a low tide this area is inaccessible.

A number of boats are moored in the area just off the beach, which should be avoided by day. However, by night, when green-headed moray eels, butterfly cod and coral shrimps emerge to feed, it provides a fantastic spectacle.

If you are lucky enough to visit the Bay at the right time of year, it is also the perfect place to view the mass coral spawning, a three-day event that begins a week or so after the full moon during the months of March and April. Check with the CALM office at Exmouth or local dive shop for the exact dates. During this spectacular nocturnal event, many species of coral suddenly release millions of mainly bright-pink egg and sperm bundles which float to the surface of the water. Mass spawning is a mechanism to ensure successful reproduction, as predators are swamped with an excess of food over a short period. The phenomenon was only discovered in 1984.

Caution areas: Beware of boat traffic. Keep clear of catfish and lionfish.
Degree of difficulty: Easy.
Area's status: Sanctuary zone within the Ningaloo Marine Park.

Peter Harding and Helene Plummer, with the assistance of Coral Dive

BUTTERFLYFISH

Many spectacular species of butterflyfish are found on Australia's tropical coral reefs. Their delightful appearance is no accident, but designed to increase their chances of mating and defining their territory. They rely on coral reefs for shelter and protection and coral polyps are also a major source of food.

There are at least 116 species of butterflyfish, which can be distinguished by the variations in their markings. However, they all have flattened bodies which enable them to squeeze in to crevices and between branches of coral. They often hover upside down, and use their fine, bristle-like teeth to nip off tasty morsels of coral. Their snouts are usually pointed, making them useful for consuming coral polyps, sponges, marine worms and perhaps small shellfish.

Most also have false eyes on their rear and a dark band over their real eyes. This subterfuge is designed to confuse predators, such as eels, scorpionfish and sea-snakes, and prevent them from attacking the vulnerable eye area. Fortunately for divers, butterflyfish tend to be active during the day but hide by night to avoid their enemies. Some species may even change colour at night to help avoid detection.

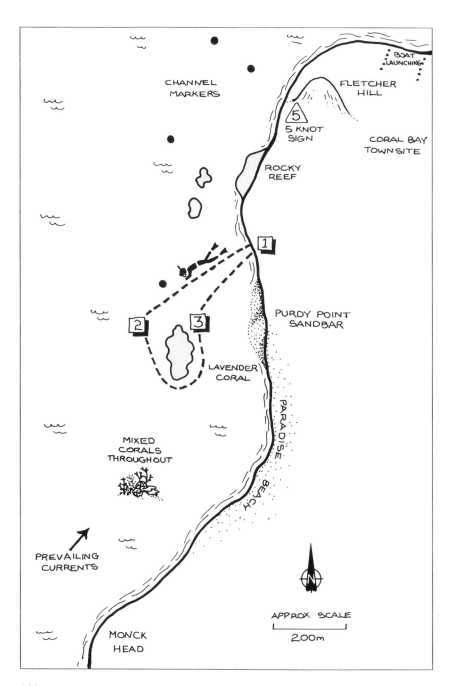

BOAT LAUNCHING

FLETCHER HILL

CHANNEL MARKERS

5 KNOT SIGN

CORAL BAY TOWNSITE

ROCKY REEF

1

PURDY POINT SANDBAR

2

3

LAVENDER CORAL

PARADISE BEACH

MIXED CORALS THROUGHOUT

PREVAILING CURRENTS

N

APPROX SCALE
200m

MONCK HEAD

Paradise Beach

37

How to get there: *Walk south along the beach from Coral Bay and then swim out 200 metres.*
Depth: *3 metres.*

This area provides reasonably safe and spectacular snorkelling which can easily be done by drifting with the surface current. A 30-minute walk south along the beach and then a 200-metre swim provides an effortless drift snorkel over magnificent coral gardens. This area is generally three metres deep, but you should exercise care over the staghorn coral, which is dense and grows close to the surface. It is best to snorkel around rather than over these areas so as to avoid damaging the fragile formations.

1. Enter the water just before you reach the sand bank at Purdy Point. To your right is an area of reef which is exposed at low tides.
2. Swim about 200 metres from the shore, taking care to avoid any boat traffic (always use a dive flag). The idea is to drift back to shore examining the diverse marine life of the area, which is packed with corals.
3. This area also has the largest patch of lavender coral around Coral Bay. It stretches for 50 metres and allows good viewing of many of the very colourful tropical reef fish. Larger wrasse, such as hump-headed wrasse and tripletail maori wrasse, are frequently seen. Two large parrotfish species, Schlegel's parrotfish and blue-barred parrotfish, often team with convict surgeonfish to form schools of 30 or 40. The surgeonfish have bold black bars on their sides and sharp spines on each side of their tail base. Many species of parrotfish exude a remarkable, mucous-like bubble in which they spend the night. It may help prevent predators from smelling them. Territorial fish, such as blue angelfish, and various species of damselfish, such as humbugs, are also seen. You may be lucky enough to spot the occasional baby reef shark. Octopuses are often seen, swimming along in mid-water.

Caution areas: *Beware of boat traffic and currents, and avoid delicate corals.*
Degree of difficulty: *Moderate. Distance from shore, nearby boat traffic, currents and lack of rest spots require a reasonable level of diving and swimming skills.*
Area's status: *Sanctuary zone within the Ningaloo Marine Park. Look but don't touch. All marine life within sanctuary zones is protected.*

Peter Harding and Helene Plummer, with assistance from Coral Dive

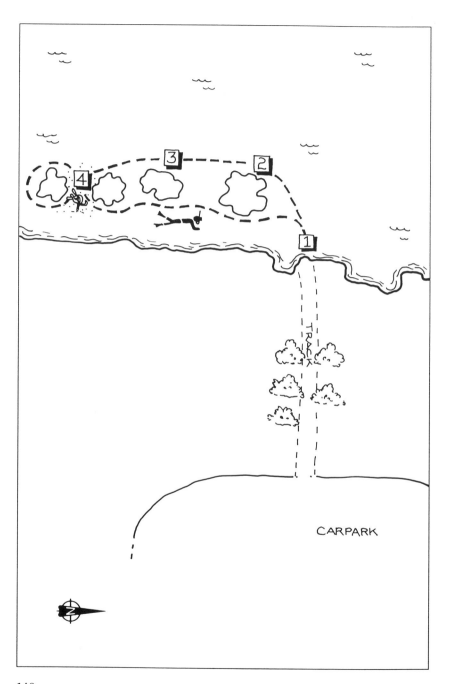

Oyster Stacks South

38

How to get there: The Oyster Stacks carpark is 12 kilometres south of the Milyering Visitor Centre in Cape Range National Park.
Depth: 2 metres at high tide.

The Oyster Stacks are five isolated islets that protrude from the reef. They are literally covered with oysters. This site should only be snorkelled on a high tide when there is sufficient water over the reef. It is best undertaken by more experienced divers. The dive around the Oyster Stacks is about 500 metres.

1. Intertidal inhabitants such as nudibranchs, clams, sea cucumbers, urchins and crabs can be seen between the rocky shoreline and the edge of the reef.
2. You can see small patches of coral belonging to the genus *Acropora*, which can adopt many guises. Different *Acropora* species such as staghorn, bush-like, plate-like, column-like and tabular forms grow here in lush profusion. These closely-related corals make up the dominant proportion of corals you will see on this dive. Each lump has its own resident mix of damselfish, chromis, butterflyfish and wrasse, varying with the size of the lump and the amount of available shelter.
3. Around the five limestone stacks are many crevices used by colourful reef fish. Sergeant major damselfish swim together in small groups. Moorish idols can be distinguished by their elongated snouts, long and unusually shaped dorsal fins and black, yellow and white colouring. Batfish are also found in the area. They have deep, nearly circular bodies and long, flowing fins. Young batfish have particularly long fins and they often mimic dead leaves by swimming on their sides. Also keep your eyes open for triggerfish, parrotfish and reef sharks. These are generally not dangerous to divers, as long as they are left alone.
4. A stretch of sandy bottom between the third and fourth stack is sparsely covered with algae. An old mooring rope, possibly used in earlier days when boats came in to the area to fish, is now covered with sea life.

Caution areas: Take care of sharp oyster shells on the stacks. Do not negotiate swimthroughs, as you could easily be cut. The shore is covered with sharp and slippery rocks, broken coral and shells, so wear appropriate footwear.
Degree of difficulty: Moderate.
Area's status: Sanctuary zone within the Ningaloo Marine Park.

Robert Thorn

149

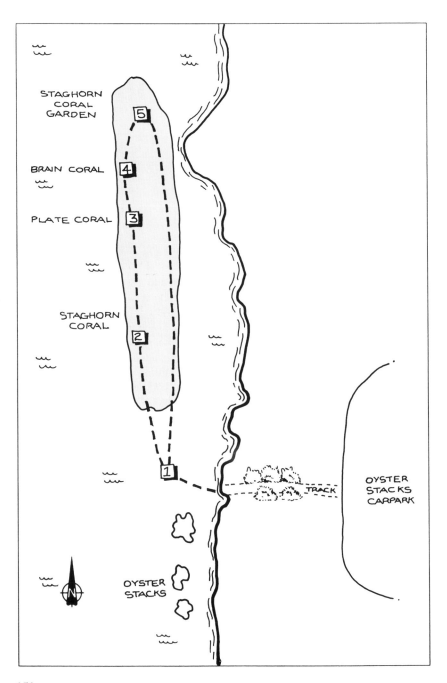

Oyster Stacks North

39

How to get there: *The Oyster Stacks carpark is 12 kilometres south of the Milyering Visitor Centre in Cape Range National Park.*
Depth: *2 metres at high tide.*

This is a fantastic dive. It has a greater diversity of staghorn corals than the Oyster Stacks South dive. You will pass through different underwater habitats of an array of coral species.

1. Enter the water adjacent to the pathway, swim straight out about 30 to 50 metres and slowly drift north with the current. From around this point you will see small patches of blue staghorn coral. Some patches of this coral have been eaten by the marine snail drupella, which has a knobbly pink shell that grows to the size of a 50 cent piece. It is found naturally at Ningaloo Reef but its numbers have exploded here. The phenomenon is similar to infestations of the crown of thorns starfish on the Great Barrier Reef.
2. Drifting along, you are likely to encounter various species of damselfish, including sergeant majors and neon damsels. Very small, brightly-coloured blue damselfish swim in small schools above the corals and retreat back in to hiding spots when you pass over them.
3. Beyond the staghorn coral there is a small area of plate coral. Many of these plates have fallen on to their sides, an indication of just how fragile they are.
4. The next habitat is an area of brightly-coloured brain coral. Brain and honey-comb corals (*Goniastera* species) are closely related.
5. The next section is dominated by a garden of blue staghorn coral. A huge range of colourful reef fish reside here. Return the way you came. If you time your dive so that it meets the high point of high tide, you should not have to swim against much of a current. If it becomes taxing, you can swim to the shore and walk back along the shoreline.

Caution areas: *The shoreline is slippery and covered with sharp rocks, broken coral and shells, so wear appropriate footwear and take care.*
Degree of difficulty: *Easy.*
Area's status: *Sanctuary zone within the Ningaloo Marine Park. Look but don't touch. All marine life in sanctuary zones is protected.*

Robert Thorn

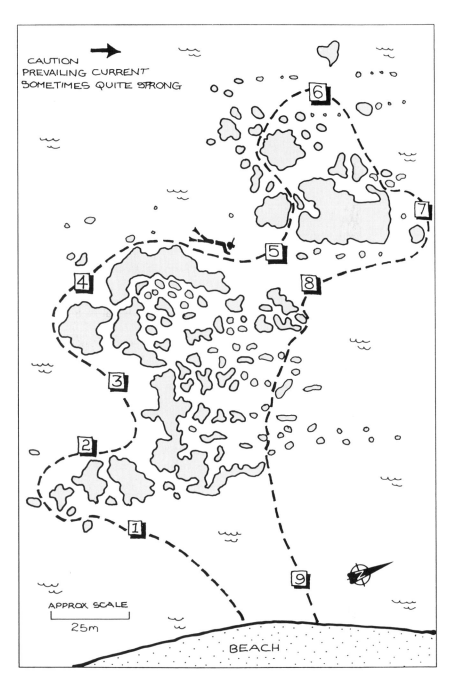

CAUTION
PREVAILING CURRENT
SOMETIMES QUITE STRONG

APPROX SCALE
25m

BEACH

Lakeside Bombies

40

How to get there*: Walk 500 metres along the beach from the Lakeside campsite in Cape Range National Park.*
Depth*: 2-5 metres during a large high tide.*

This shore dive is a good spot for snorkellers. Lakeside has numerous bombies of massive corals (*Porites* species), but many other kinds of coral also grow in the area. The corals feed on tiny plankton produced in the clear, warm ocean. They are themselves eaten by and shelter a profusion of other marine life, including many colourful and beautifully-patterned fish. However, the site can experience quite strong currents due to tidal movements and large swells breaking over the main reef crest, one and a half skilometres offshore. These can create lagoonal currents seeking a route back to sea through gaps in the reef. Plan to dive at slack tide and be cautious of currents if the main reef has large swells breaking over it.

If you stop at Milyering Visitor Centre in Cape Range National Park to check on tides and weather conditions, staff will be able to give you directions to the site. From the visitor centre carpark, take the access road that leads towards the beach, then turn south at a T-junction to Lakeside campsite. Park adjacent to the campsite, but note that vehicle access is not allowed along the beach north or south of the sandbar. You must walk south along the beach for 500 metres to reach the entry point.

1. Schools of surgeonfish, parrotfish, dart and trevally can often be seen here. Some paddleweed seagrass grows on the sandy bottom.
2. Numerous small reef fish and invertebrates inhabit an area containing small to medium-sized corals and algae-covered rock. Large rays are commonly seen on the adjacent sandy bottom.
3. A small broken coral wall with interesting ledges progresses in to a bombie wall. You should be able to locate an isolated medium coral head, with a huge anemone colony and its symbiotic anemonefish. These bright orange and white fish have developed a mucous that prevents the anemone's stinging tentacles from triggering. These small fish then gain protection from predatory fish by retreating into the tentacles.
4. A coral wall with a ledge at its base often harbours stingrays, angelfish, toadfish, goatfish and other fish species. The small staghorn corals on top generally have drupella consuming them. These small, knobbly marine snails strip the living veneer of coral from the reef. They have eaten out large areas of Ningaloo.

5. The next point of interest is a sandy gutter with scattered stands of fire coral. This is not a true coral. Take care not to brush against it, as this species can cause a burning sensation. Large schools of pike, juvenile snapper, trevally, toadfish, surgeonfish and parrotfish frequent the area.
6. The southern face of a massive coral has several caves and crevices in which you can often see sharks and rays dozing. Massive corals are fairly slow-growing. Colonies four metres high may be more than 500 years old and therefore could have been growing long before Europeans came to Australia. There are numerous coral heads of various sizes on the seaward side.
7. There is a bombora wall with an isolated bombie on the north-east corner. The main bombie is flat-topped and has extremely diverse reef fauna.
8. A ledge at the base of a wall of coral is a favourite spot for rays and toadfish. As you move back towards shore, you will swim over clouds of chromis fish hovering above stands of fire coral.
9. On the way back to shore you may see a number of small coral colonies of various species amongst rocky rubble and algae. Anemones, sea cucumbers, urchins, turban shells, clams and burrowing fish are commonly seen.

Caution areas: *The prevailing current is sometimes quite strong. Beware of fireweed, fire coral, stingrays, toadfish, stonefish and sea urchins.*
Degree of difficulty: *Easy to moderately difficult, depending on conditions.*
Area's status: *Lies within the Ningaloo Marine Park.*

Rick Karniewicz

WHALE SHARKS

Whale sharks (*Rhincodon typus*) are the world's biggest species of fish. These magnificent animals are generally between four and 12 metres long, but they are harmless to people. Faced with an animal this size looming out of the ocean, a diver's first view of a whale shark is a heart-stopping experience. It is impossible not to marvel at their sheer power and beauty, and their huge bodies patterned with rows of white spots. Divers are well-advised to keep clear of their enormous tails.

The gentle giants are believed to be migratory and begin to appear in large numbers at Ningaloo Marine Park, near Exmouth, from mid-March to mid-May each year. Their appearance is related to the mass spawning of the reef's corals, a time when a huge amount of food is available in the water. They are thought to be feeding on krill, plankton and small schooling fish, rather than the coral spawn itself.

Scientists from the CSIRO Division of Fisheries in Hobart recently attached archival tags to six whale sharks. The tags can collect data for up to five years and store it for 20 years. Each tag has an accurate time clock, as well as depth, light and temperature sensors. They collect information that shows the time of sunrise and sunset, from which the latitude and longitude of the whale's location can be accurately worked out. If one or more of these tags can be recovered, scientists will have a huge amount of information on the distances travelled, where the sharks go and the depths to which they dive.

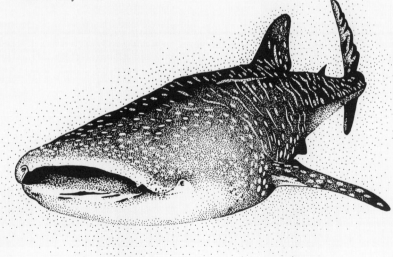

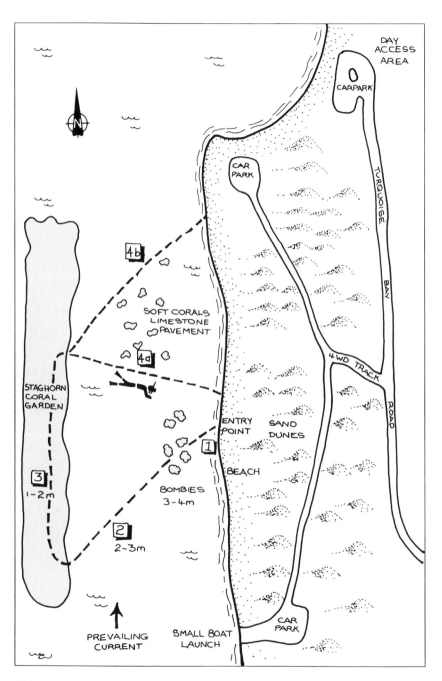

DAY ACCESS AREA

CARPARK

CAR PARK

TURQUOISE BAY

4 WD TRACK

ROAD

4b

SOFT CORALS
LIMESTONE
PAVEMENT

4a

STAGHORN
CORAL
GARDEN

ENTRY
POINT

SAND
DUNES

1

BEACH

3
1-2m

BOMBIES
3-4m

2
2-3m

PREVAILING
CURRENT

SMALL BOAT
LAUNCH

CAR
PARK

N

Turquoise Bay - southern drift

41

How to get there: Turquoise Bay is 10 kilometres south of the Milyering Visitor Centre in Cape Range National Park and 65 kilometres from Exmouth.
Depth: Up to 4 metres.

The coral bombies close to shore are suited to most skill levels, making this an excellent family dive. However, the prevailing northerly current can be quite strong, so the swim out to the staghorn coral garden can be taxing. Inexperienced or younger divers should only dive on the staghorn coral garden in good conditions and under the supervision of a more experienced person. The site can be dived on either snorkel or SCUBA, although the staghorn coral garden is very shallow and you will be on the surface no matter what breathing apparatus you have.

To get to the dive site, drive down the four-wheel-drive track off the main Turquoise Bay access road. To protect the environment and minimise disturbance to other beach users, please do not drive vehicles along the beach any further than the parking areas. Walk down the dune access track to the beach and walk southwards along the beach for about 30 to 40 metres to the entry point. If you do not have a four-wheel-drive, drive to the end of the Turquoise Bay road and park in the day access area. Walk to the beach and south around the point to the dive entry point.

1. A short swim across a sandy bottom will bring you to some bombies. Swim in a west-south-westerly direction against the prevailing current. The sandy bottom is a favourite haunt for rays, spangled emperor (also known as north-west snapper) and dart. Sea cucumbers can be seen feeding on the bottom. Around the bombies you are likely to see numerous species of reef fish, including parrotfish, wrasse and butterflyfish. Look under ledges for resting rays and cod.
2. Continue swimming south-west and slightly in to the current for 150 to 200 metres, passing over sandy rubble, with occasional outcrops of soft and fire corals. Keep an eye out for larger fish such as spangled emperor, rays and schools of buffalo bream. The distinctive wavy shells and blue-green mantles of clams can also be seen.
3. After the sandy area you will reach a staghorn coral garden. This is a shallow coral area with numerous species of fish. Allow yourself to drift northwards with the current. The branches of staghorn coral will break easily so avoid touching them. Many fish are found amongst the staghorn. Look under ledges for resting white-

tipped reef sharks, rays and batfish. Check your location periodically as you drift north.

4. To avoid swimming against the current, start to angle back towards the shore before you reach a point just north-west of the dune access track. Depending on the location of your vehicle, you can swim slightly in to the current and end up back at the dune access track or head to the north-east with the current and come out at the day access area. During the swim you may see outcrops of soft corals and limestone pavement. Look out for a variety of reef fish around the coral outcrops and burrowing fish guarding their homes on the sandy bottom.

Caution areas: Keep clear of stingrays, fire coral, fireweed, stonefish and coneshells.
Degree of difficulty: Moderate. Unless you confine your dive to the inshore bombies, a reasonable level of fitness and diving skill is required.
Area's status: Sanctuary zone within the Ningaloo Marine Park. Look but don't touch. All marine life within sanctuary zones is protected.

Fran Burbidge

DIFFERENT TYPES OF CORAL

It is the way in which corals lay down their supporting skeleton, and bud and divide to form colonies, that gives rise to the great diversity of form found in reef colonies. At Ningaloo Marine Park, for instance, there are more than 220 different species of corals. Most hard coral colonies have been formed as a result of asexual reproduction, beginning with a single polyp dividing to produce two individuals, which in turn divide to continue the process.

Massive corals (*Porites* species) often form enormous domes. Some of the very large massive colonies may have begun to form centuries ago, and consist of thousands of individual polyps, each one a genetic replica of the original single ancestor. Brain corals have polyps that divide without making completely separate walls, forming long, meandering lines of polyps along a bulbous lump formed by their skeletons. The staghorn, or branching corals (*Acropora* species) have single large polyps at the tips of their branches, which grow longer as the branches elongate and bud off smaller polyps at their edges. They favour fairly sheltered lagoons that protect the delicate structures they have created. On deeper parts of the reef, sprawling plate-like forms maximise capture of the limited available light.

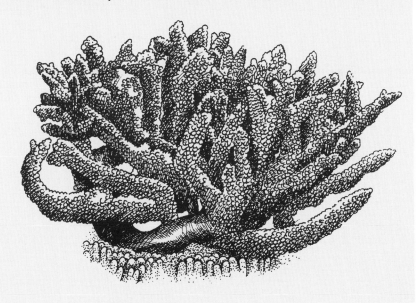

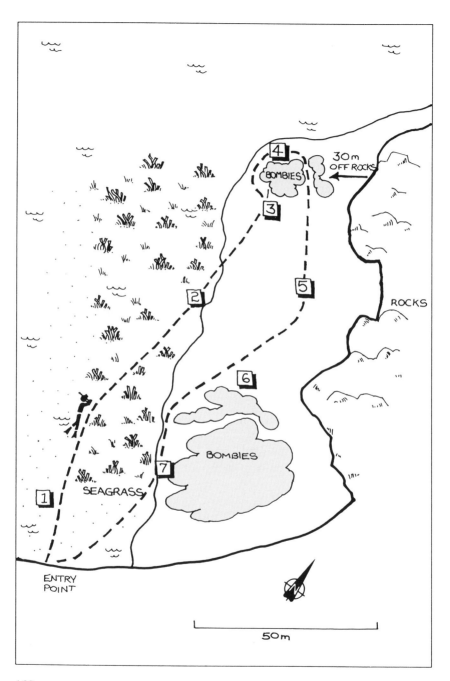

Turquoise Bay brain coral   **42**

How to get there: Turquoise Bay is 10 kilometres south of Milyering Visitor Centre in Cape Range National Park and 65 kilometres from Exmouth.
Depth: 2 metres.

This is an excellent dive site for the family because of its ease in most conditions, the rich diversity of coral, fish and other marine life very close to shore and the exceptional beauty of the beach and Turquoise Bay itself.

The access road to Turquoise Bay from Yardie Creek will lead you to the main carpark at the elbow of the bay. From the beach in front of the carpark, walk north for about 200 metres. Alternatively, if you have a four-wheel-drive, you can turn north in to a spur road about halfway between Yardie Creek Road and the carpark. The spur road leads to Camp 19, a small camping area. Walk 50 metres south from the shoreline adjacent to the campsite.

1. Enter the water at the point where the clear sandy bottom meets the shadowed area of reef and weed. Follow the edge of the weedy area in a north to north-westerly direction. See if you can spot sea cucumbers, sea urchins, small clams and other invertebrates sheltering in the seaweeds and seagrasses.

2. Continue north along the transition line between the reef shelf and the seaweed and seagrass-dominated bottom. This will lead you to several large coral bombies. Many species of colourful reef fish live in and around these colonies of massive coral. The myriad of angelfish, wrasse and parrotfish in different shapes, sizes and colours are a delight to watch. Parrotfish are closely related to wrasse, but have dental plates which give them beak-like mouths. Like wrasse, they change sex from females to males.

3. Moving along the reef you will encounter numerous small coral colonies, particularly brain and slow-growing massive corals. The water is shallow here, only between one to one and a half metres deep.

4. There are several large bombies to explore, about 50 metres from the rocky shore. Numerous brain corals grow around them.

5 & 6. On the way back, inspect two patches of staghorn coral. They are extremely fragile and easily broken, so avoid touching them.

7. It is best to swim around the rocky outcrops, as there is usually little water over them. There are many small holes beneath the ledges, which are used by large, colourful reef fish for shelter.

Caution areas: *If the main reef is experiencing large swells, heavy seas and/or extreme tides, there may be strong currents or other hazardous conditions at the site. Keep clear of stingrays, fire coral, fireweed, stonefish and coneshells.*
Degree of difficulty: *Easy.*
Area's status: *Sanctuary zone within the Ningaloo Marine Park.*

Robert Thorn and Ric Karniewicz

SEA-SNAKES

For air-breathing animals, sea-snakes are remarkable divers. Some species can dive to 100 metres or more, and remain submerged for up to two hours. This may be partly due to the ability of some species to absorb part of the oxygen they need through their skins. Sea-snakes are adapted to breathe, feed, breed and grow in the sea. For instance, their flat tail acts as a paddle to help them swim more effectively.

Sea-kraits are closely related to sea-snakes, but differ from true sea-snakes by laying eggs and sometimes landing to lay eggs and rest. True sea-snakes give birth to live young in the sea. Although both sea-snakes and sea-kraits are highly venomous, they rarely attack people unless provoked and, even when they do, they do not always release venom. The venom is used to subdue and kill prey, which is then grabbed in the jaws and swallowed whole. The skullbones of snakes are loosely attached and they can dislocate their lower jaws and slide them sideways to allow them to swallow their prey. They tend to be fussy eaters. Some only eat catfish, another the eggs of only two families of fish. Others enjoy eels, fish, prawns, crabs and worms.

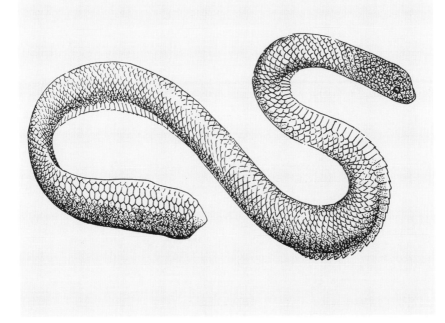

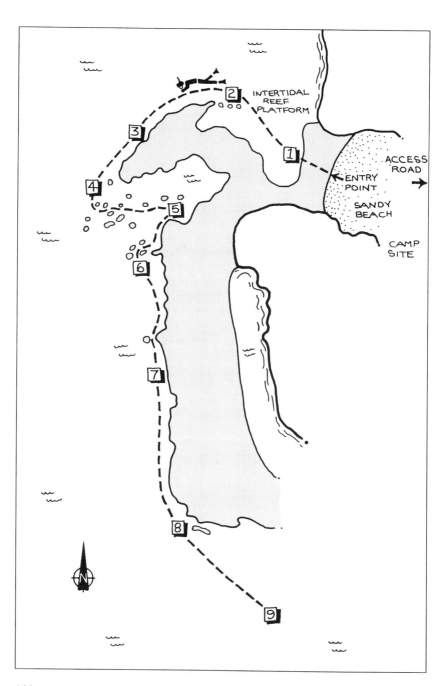

INTERTIDAL
REEF
PLATFORM

ACCESS
ROAD

ENTRY
POINT

SANDY
BEACH

CAMP
SITE

N

Pilgramunna Ledges

How to get there: Drive 72 kilometres from Exmouth to the Pilgramunna turn-off, from which there is a short walk to the beach.
Depth: 3-4 metres at high tide.

This is an excellent dive for families and divers of any level. You can drive your vehicle close to the entry point and the dive is undemanding, with the diver rarely more than 10 metres from shore and only swimming about 150 metres in total. Despite this, the site has a surprising diversity of marine life, some beautiful coral formations, multitudes of colourful reef fish, occasional oceanic fish species, as well as rays, sharks and diverse invertebrates. This is the best dive around for obtaining maximum reward for minimum effort. Inexperienced divers may need to be accompanied and the site should not be dived if unsuitable conditions prevail (see note below). It is best dived on a high tide when the intertidal reef platforms are covered.

On the way you may like to stop at the Milyering Visitor Centre, which is 50 kilometres from Exmouth in Cape Range National Park. Proceed south for another 22 kilometres to the turn-off to Pilgramunna campsite. The campsite is within a miniature cove, with a small sandy beach extended well back from shore. Park near the campsite, taking care not to drive over any vegetation. Tides can intrude well into the campsite, so park behind the high tide line. The entry point is right opposite the campsite.

1. Just beyond the sandy beach there is an area of intertidal reef platform. Blue-spotted stingrays are commonly seen in the lagoon, along with invertebrates such as clams, sea cucumbers and sea urchins.
2. Around the many bombies you can see sea urchins, boxfish, Moorish idols, schools of fusilier and regal angelfish, which are often seen in pairs and may mate for life.
3. Drummers, large wrasse, parrotfish and long-finned batfish can be seen swimming amongst the brain coral and diverse species of staghorn coral.
4. Large plate coral, large brain coral and a very large blue staghorn coral grow in the area. Damselfish, Moorish idols and sea urchins can be seen in and around them.
5. Swim in to the lagoon. It is recommended that you enter this area during high tide.
6. Numerous reef fish can be seen, as well as large plate corals and brain corals. Other colourful inhabitants of this area include damselfish and blue-girdled

angelfish. Wedge-tailed triggerfish can be seen. They have a wedge-shaped marking on their tails and may grunt when disturbed. Cardinalfish are also found here. They are remarkable in that the males incubate the egg masses in their mouths. Red squirrelfish shelter under ledges and in caves by day, emerging at night to hunt for fish.

7. Explore the ledges along the intertidal reef platform. The crevices on the bottom shelter large fish and, sometimes, sleeping leopard sharks. They are harmless and have leopard-like spots and oversized tails.
8. Snorkel around numerous rocky ledges and bombies, where you can view a variety of large fish, including boxfish and blue-girdled angelfish.
9. On a section of sandy bottom you may see blue-spotted stingrays, clams and nudibranchs. You can either leave the water and walk back or snorkel back along the same route.

Caution areas: The site should not be dived if large swells or seas are breaking or causing a turbulent wash on the front of the rock ledges. Keep clear of catfish, fire corals, stinging hydroids, stonefish and coneshells.
Degree of difficulty: *Easy.*
Area's status: *Lies within the Ningaloo Marine Park.*

Robert Thorn

FISHY TRANSVESTITES

Members of the tropical damselfish family make a rather drastic transformation when a member of their social group dies. They don't just mourn - one of them actually has a sex change. Anemonefish, for example, live in groups of one large dominant female and one or more smaller males. Only the largest male fertilises the female's eggs, as the others are sterile. Size and the aggressive behaviour of each fish towards those below it (with the female at the top of the pecking order) maintain the hierarchy. However, the males' testes contain rudimentary ovaries. If the female dies, the largest male begins to act like a female and develops fully functioning ovaries. At the same time, the second-largest male becomes sexually mature and takes over as the dominant male. The remainder of male anemonefish stay sterile.

On the other hand, the humbug, or reticulated dascyllus, lives in groups of up to 100 individuals. The largest fish is always a male, and he dominates a large harem of females. He chases all other males from his territory to ensure only he can fertilise the females' eggs. If he dies, the largest female begins to behave like a male. Before long, she loses her ovaries, develops male sex organs and begins to father new broods.